OVER 120
CROCHET
FLOWERS & BLOCKS
FABULOUS MOTIFS AND FLOWERS

Tuva Publishing
www.tuvapublishing.com

Address Merkez Mah. Cavusbasi Cad. No:71
Cekmekoy - Istanbul 34782 / Turkey
Tel: +9 0216 642 62 62

Crochet Flowers & Blocks

First Print 2019 / April

Content Crochet
Editor in Chief Ayhan DEMİRPEHLİVAN
Project Editor Kader DEMİRPEHLİVAN
Technical Editors Wendi CUSINS, Leyla ARAS, Büşra ESER
Graphic Designers Ömer ALP, Abdullah BAYRAKÇI, Zilal ÖNEL
Photography Tuva Publishing

ISBN 978-605-9192-82-8

Basıldığı Matbaa
Uniprint Basım San. ve Tic. AŞ.

INTRODUCTION

In this book you will find a fabulous collection of crochet flowers and motif blocks. With this host of lovely modern crochet blooms and blocks, you will be able to make a stunning range of items, both small and large, including blankets, shawls, throws, tote bags, cushions, doilies, scarves, hats and even jumpers. From the humble traditional granny square to delicate triangle motifs, you can get creative to combine blocks and flowers to design your own, stylish projects and makes.

The book is divided into two main sections: Flowers and Blocks. The Flower section contains flowers and leaves whilst the Blocks section has a variety of different shaped motifs including triangles, hexagons, circles and squares.

The Flowers can be used as stunning embellishments for ready made items or to add that extra finishing touch to your own makes from clothes to accessories, soft furnishings and homewares. We have included lots of ideas to inspire you on how to use the Flowers and Blocks to make some extra special items.

The instructions for all Flowers and Blocks are written using US crochet terms and are accompanied by crochet charts and. The samples in the book were made using the DMC Natura yarn family - DMC Natura Just Cotton, DMC Natura Medium and DMC Natura XL. Natura is a lovely soft cotton yarn that comes in a range of different weights and shades for use with all of the patterns in the book. But you can also try out all of these motifs with any yarn you prefer to use!

With more than 120 crochet blocks and flowers motifs to choose from, there really is something for crocheters of every skill level. We hope you enjoy using this motif book to make your own bespoke crochet designs for yourself and your family and friends.

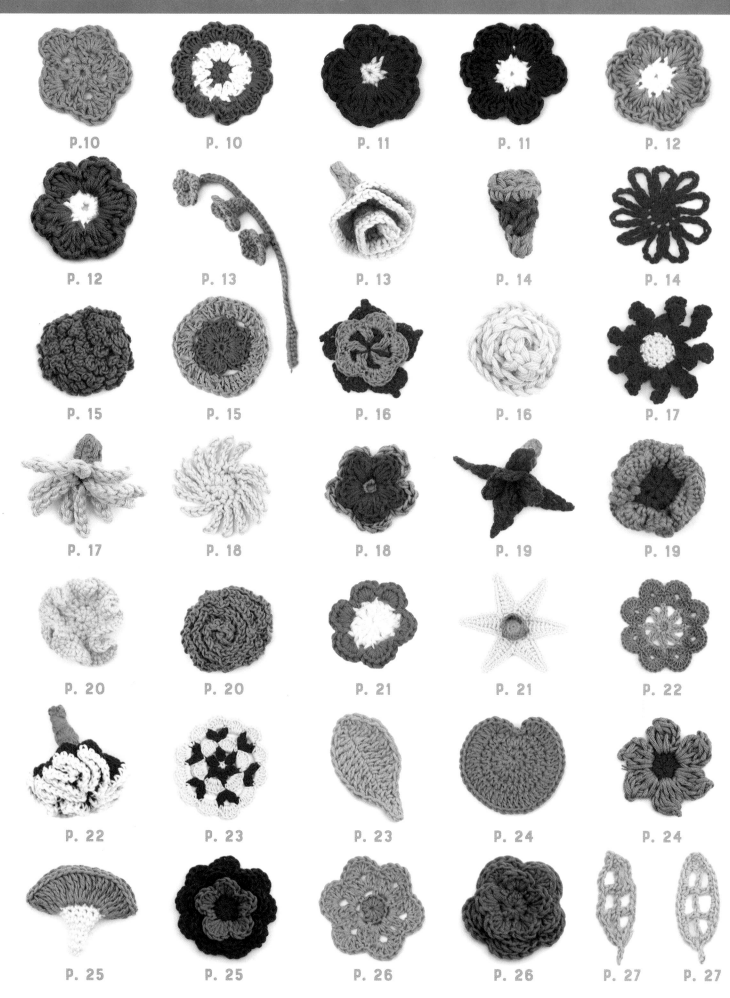

P.10   P.10   P.11   P.11   P.12

P. 12   P. 13   P. 13   P. 14   P. 14

P. 15   P. 15   P. 16   P. 16   P. 17

P. 17   P. 18   P. 18   P. 19   P. 19

P. 20   P. 20   P. 21   P. 21   P. 22

P. 22   P. 23   P. 23   P. 24   P. 24

P. 25   P. 25   P. 26   P. 26   P. 27   P. 27

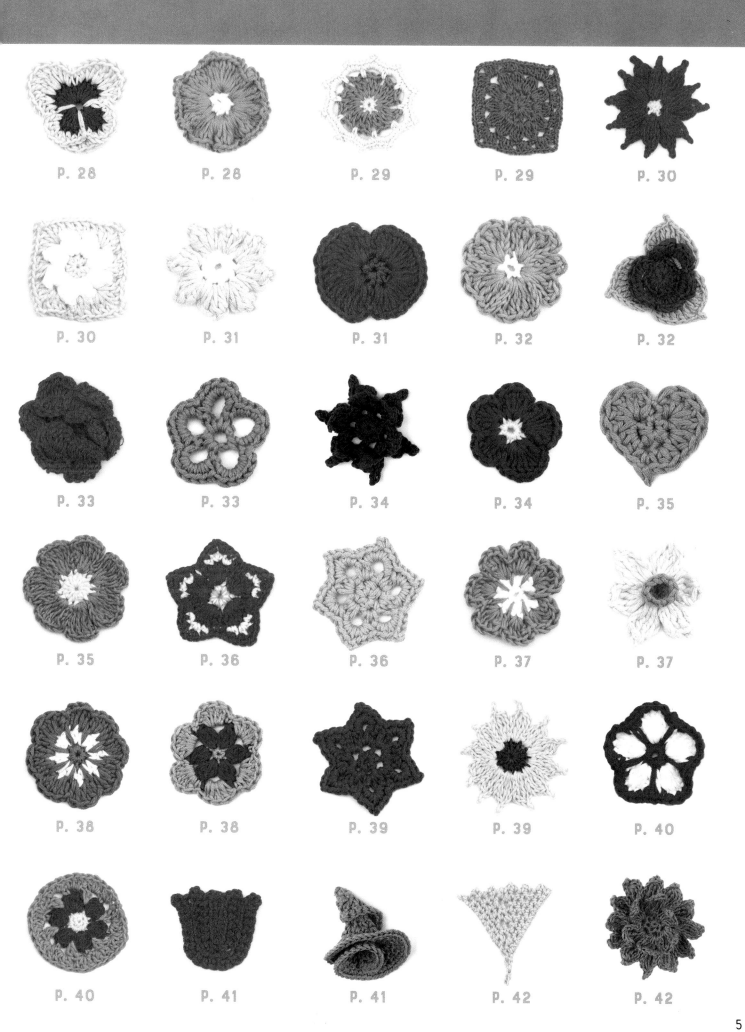

P. 28　　　P. 28　　　P. 29　　　P. 29　　　P. 30

P. 30　　　P. 31　　　P. 31　　　P. 32　　　P. 32

P. 33　　　P. 33　　　P. 34　　　P. 34　　　P. 35

P. 35　　　P. 36　　　P. 36　　　P. 37　　　P. 37

P. 38　　　P. 38　　　P. 39　　　P. 39　　　P. 40

P. 40　　　P. 41　　　P. 41　　　P. 42　　　P. 42

5

P.46 P.47 P.48 P.49 P.50

P.51 P.52 P.53 P.54 P.55

P.56 P.57 P.58 P.59 P.60

P.61 P.62 P.63 P.64 P.65

P.66 P.67 P.68 P.69 P.70

P.71 P.72 P.73 P.74 P.75

FLOWERS
66 FLOWERS AND LEAVES

FLOWER 1 — 5 Petal Wheel Center Motif

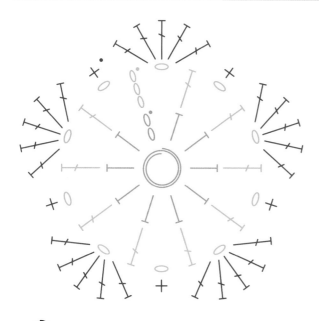

PATTERN

ROUND 1: MR, ch 2, 9 hdc, join with sl st.

ROUND 2: Ch 4 (counts as 1 dc and ch-1), (1 dc, ch 1) in each hdc, join with sl st in 3rd ch of beg ch-4.

ROUND 3: (1 sc in ch-1 sp, 5 dc in foll ch-1 sp) 5 times, join with sl st. Fasten off, weave in ends.

⭕ **MR -** magic ring	**hdc -** half double crochet
◯ **ch -** chain	
• **sl st -** slip stitch	**dc -** double crochet
✛ **sc -** single crochet	

FLOWER 2 — Two Color Round Flower

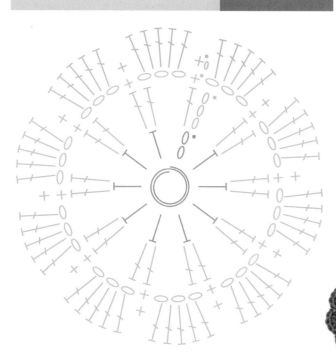

PATTERN

ROUND 1: In color A, MR, ch 2, 9 hdc in ring, join with sl st, fasten off.

ROUND 2: Join color B in any st, (ch 3, 1 dc) in same st, * 2 dc in next st; rep from * 8 times more, join with sl st in top of ch-3, fasten off.

ROUND 3: Using Color A, join with sc to any st, (ch3, skip 1 st, 1 sc in next st) 9 times, ch 3, join with sl st.

ROUND 4: Ch 1, sc in same st as joining, (5 dc in ch-3 sp, 1 sc in next sc) 9 times, 5 dc in ch-3 sp, join with sl st. Fasten off, weave in ends.

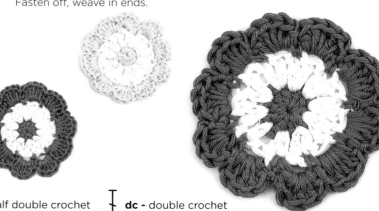

⭕ **MR -** magic ring	• **sl st -** slip stitch	**hdc -** half double crochet
◯ **ch -** chain	✛ **sc -** single crochet	**dc -** double crochet

FLOWER 3 — 5 Round Petal Flower - Small

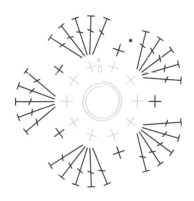

PATTERN

ROUND 1: In color A, MR, ch 1, 10 sc in ring, join with sl st, fasten off.

ROUND 2: Using color B, join with sc to any sc, * 5 dc in next st, sc in foll st; rep from * 3 times more. 5dc in next st, join with sl st to first sc. Fasten off, weave in ends.

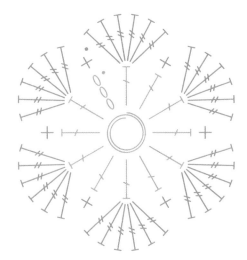

MR - magic ring

ch - chain

sl st - slip stitch

sc - single crochet

dc - double crochet

FLOWER 4 — 6 Round Petal Flower - Large

PATTERN

ROUND 1: In color A, MR, ch 3, 11 dc in ring, join with sl st, fasten off.

ROUND 2: Using color B, join with sc to any dc, * 6 tr in next st, sc in foll st; rep from * 4 times more, 6 tr in next st, join with sl st to first sc. Fasten off, weave in ends.

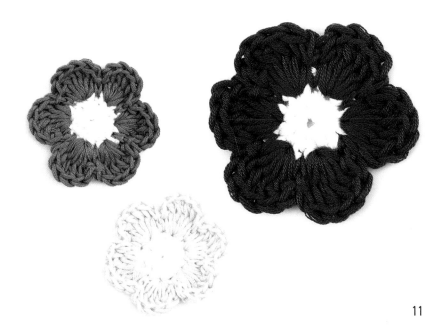

MR - magic ring

ch - chain

sl st - slip stitch

sc - single crochet

dc - double crochet

tr - treble crochet

FLOWER 5

6 Round Petal Flower - Medium

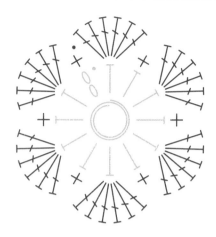

PATTERN

ROUND 1: In color A, MR, ch 2, 11 hdc in ring, join with sl st, fasten off.

ROUND 2: Using color B, join with sc to any hdc, * 5 dc in next st, sc in foll st; rep from * 4 times more, 5 dc in next st, join with sl st to first sc. Fasten off, weave in ends.

MR - magic ring	**hdc -** half double crochet
ch - chain	
sl st - slip stitch	**dc -** double crochet
sc - single crochet	

FLOWER 6

6 Round Petal Flower - Small

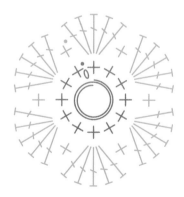

PATTERN

ROUND 1: In color A, MR, ch 1, 12 sc in ring, join with sl st, fasten off.

ROUND 2: Using color B, join with sc in any sc, * 5 dc in next st, sc in foll st; rep from * 4 times more, 5 dc in next stitch, join with sl st to first sc. Fasten off, weave in ends.

MR - magic ring

ch - chain

sl st - slip stitch

sc - single crochet

dc - double crochet

FLOWER 7 — Bluebell

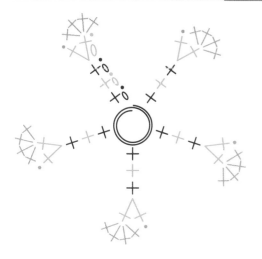

PATTERN

ROUND 1: MR, ch 1, 5 sc in ring, join with sl st.

ROUND 2: Ch 1, 1 sc in each sc, join with sl st.

ROUND 3: Rep the last round once more

ROUND 4: Ch 1, 2 sc in each sc, join with sl st.

ROUND 5: (4 sc in next st, sl st in foll st) 5 times.
Fasten off, weave in ends.

Make several of the bluebell flowers and attach them to a stem, as shown, to make a spray of flowers. Follow the instructions on page 111 to make stems.

MR - magic ring

ch - chain

sl st - slip stitch

sc - single crochet

FLOWER 8 — Carnation Flower

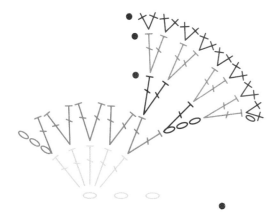

Repeat to end

PATTERN

ROW 1: In stem color, ch 3, work 5 dc in 3rd ch from hook, ch 3, turn.

ROW 2: Work 1 dc in same st as ch-3, work 2 dc in each st to end. Fasten off stem color and weave in all ends. Ch3, (change to petal color before making ch 3), turn.

ROW 3: Work 1 dc in same st as ch-3, work 2 dc in each st to end, ch 3, turn .

ROW 4: Work 1 dc in same st as ch-3, work 2 dc in each st to end. Fasten off petal color, ch 1 (change to petal edge color before making ch 1), turn.

ROW 5: Work 2 sc in each st to end.
Fasten off, weave in ends.
Roll up to form flower and sew in place.

ch - chain

sc - single crochet

dc - double crochet

13

FLOWER 9 — Carnation Bud

PATTERN

ROW 1: In stem color, ch 3, work 5 dc in 3rd ch from hook. Fasten off stem color and weave in all ends, ch 3 (change to bud color before making ch 3), turn.

ROW 2: Work 1 dc in same st as ch-3, work 2 dc in each st to end. Fasten off bud color and weave in all end, ch 1 (change to bud edge color before making ch 1), turn.

ROW 3: Work 2 sc in each st to end.

Fasten off, weave in ends.

Roll up to form bud and sew in place.

⬭ **ch -** chain

✛ **sc -** single crochet

┼ **dc -** double crochet

FLOWER 10 — Chain Flower / Daisy Chain

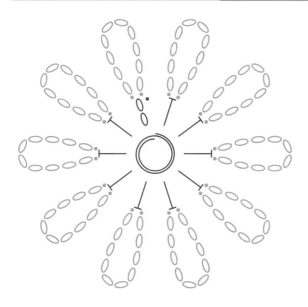

PATTERN

ROUND 1: MR, ch 2, 9 hdc in ring, join with sl st.

ROUND 2: * Ch 10, sl st in same st, sl st in next st; rep from * 9 times more.

Fasten off, weave in ends.

◯ **MR -** magic ring

⬭ **ch -** chain

● **sl st -** slip stitch

│ **hdc -** half double crochet

FLOWER 11 — Chain Squiggle Flower Base

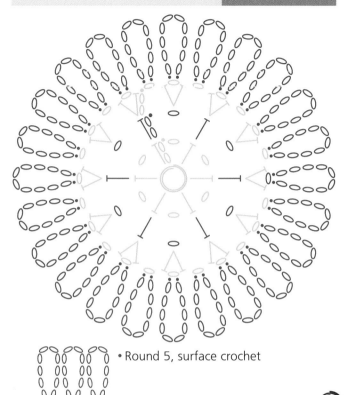

• Round 5, surface crochet

• Round 2

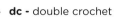

PATTERN

ROUND 1: MR, ch 2, (1 hdc, ch 1) 6 times in ring, join with sl st.

ROUND 2: Ch 2, * 1 hdc in top of hdc, ch 1, skip ch 1 in round below; rep from * 5 times more, join with sl st

ROUND 3: Ch 2, [work (1 hdc, ch 1, 1 hdc, ch 1) in each hdc and ch-1 sp] 12 times, join with sl st.

ROUND 4: Sl st in ch-1 sp, *ch 10, sl st in same ch-1 sp, sl st in next ch-1 sp; rep from * 23 more times.

Petals worked as surface crochet in the ch-1 sp in the base.

ROUND 5: Sl st in ch-1 sp in round 2, *ch 10, sl st in same ch-1 sp, sl st in next ch-1 sp; rep from * working in a spiral until all the ch-1 sps from rounds 3-1 have a chain loop worked in them.

Fasten off, weave in ends.

MR - magic ring

○ **ch** - chain

● **sl st** - slip stitch

| **hdc** - half double crochet

FLOWER 12 — Circled Flower Motif

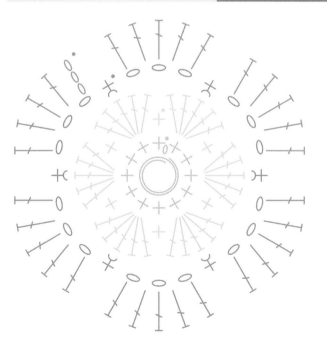

PATTERN

ROUND 1: In color A, MR, ch 1, 12 sc in ring, join with sl st.

ROUND 2: * Work 1 sc in next sc, 5 dc in foll sc; rep from * 5 times more, fasten off color A.

ROUND 3: Using color B, working in blo, sc in 3rd dc in 5-dc petal, * ch 3, sc in blo of 3rd dc of next 5-dc petal; rep from * 5 times more.

ROUND 4: Sl st in next ch-3 sp, (ch 3, 4 dc) in same sp, * 5 dc in next ch-3 sp; rep from * 4 times more, join with sl st in top of ch-3.

Fasten off, weave in ends.

MR - magic ring

● **sl st** - slip stitch

| **dc** - double crochet

○ **ch** - chain

+ **sc** - single crochet

╬ sc in back loop

FLOWER 13 — Clematis

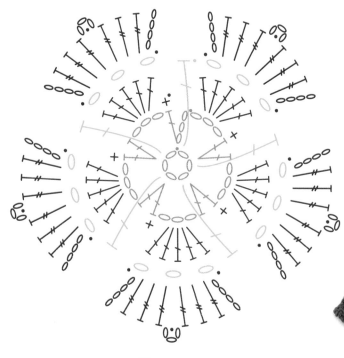

PATTERN

Base Round: In center color, ch 6, join with sl st to form a ring.

ROUND 1: Ch 3, 1 dc, ch 3, (2 dc, ch 3) 4 times in ring, join with sl st in top of first ch-3.

ROUND 2: Work sc in next st, (5 dc in next ch-3 sp, skip 1 st, 1 sc in next st) 4 times, 5 dc in next ch-3 sp, join with sl st to first sc, fasten off.

ROUND 3: Join outer color to back of dc from round 3, working behind the petals, (long dc in ring of round 1 between 2 dc from round 2, ch 3) 5 times, sl st to first long dc.

ROUND 4: (Sl st in next ch-3 sp, ch 4, 3 tr, ch 3 picot, 3 tr, ch 4, sl st in same sp) 5 times.
Fasten off, weave in ends.

⬭ **ch** - chain	Ọ.Ọ **ch 3 picot**
● **sl st** - slip stitch	+ **sc** - single crochet

⊺ **dc** - double crochet ⊧ **tr** - treble crochet | **long dc**

FLOWER 14 — Curled Bud

PATTERN

ROW 1: Ch 9, 7 dc in 3rd ch from hook, 7 dc in each ch to end.
Allow to curl and sl st in 1 dc to close the base.
Fasten off, weave in ends.

⬭ **ch** - chain ⊺ **dc** - double crochet

FLOWER 15 — Curled Petal Flower

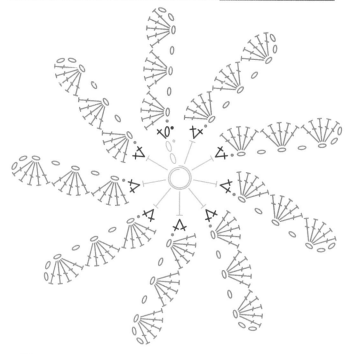

PATTERN

ROUND 1: In center color, MR, ch 2, 8 hdc in ring, join with sl st.

ROUND 2: Ch 1, 1 sc in same st, (2 sc in each hdc) 8 times, join with sl st.

ROUND 3: Join petal color, * ch 7, work 5 dc in 3rd ch from hook, (skip 1-ch, 5 dc in next ch) twice, skip 1 sc, sl st in next sc; rep from * 8 times more.

Fasten off, weave in ends.

MR - magic ring **+** **sc -** single crochet **dc -** double crochet

ch - chain **hdc -** half double crochet

sl st - slip stitch

FLOWER 16 — Dandelion Bud

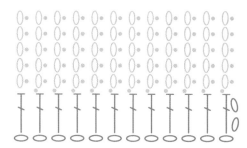

PATTERN

ROW 1: In green, ch 14, work 1 dc in 3rd ch from hook, work 1 dc in each ch to end, fasten off.

ROW 2: Join yellow, * ch 5, sl st back down ch-5, sl st in next dc; rep from * to end.

Roll up and sew in place.

Fasten off, weave in ends.

ch - chain

sl st - slip stitch

dc - double crochet

FLOWER 17 — Dandelion Flower

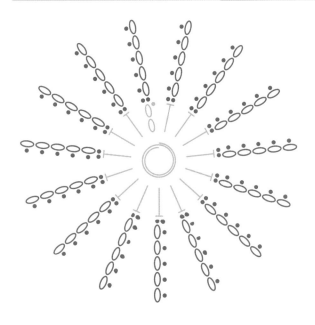

PATTERN

ROUND 1: In yellow, MR, ch 2, 14 hdc in ring, join with sl st.

ROUND 2: * Ch 5, sl st back down ch-5, sl st in next hdc; rep from * 14 times more.

Fasten off, weave in ends.

MR - magic ring	• **sl st -** slip stitch
ch - chain	**hdc -** half double crochet

FLOWER 18 — Double Flower

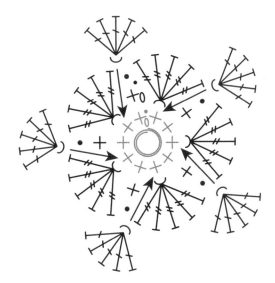

PATTERN

ROUND 1: In color A, MR, ch 1, 10 sc in ring, join with sl st.

ROUND 2: Ch 1, (1 sc in sc, 5 tr in blo of next sc) 5 times, sl st in first sc, fasten off.

ROUND 3: Join color B in flo of petal just worked, (5 dc in flo, sl st in next sc) 5 times.

Fasten off, weave in ends.

MR - magic ring	**sc -** single crochet
ch - chain	dc in front loop tr in back loop
• **sl st -** slip stitch	

18

FLOWER 19 — Fuchsia

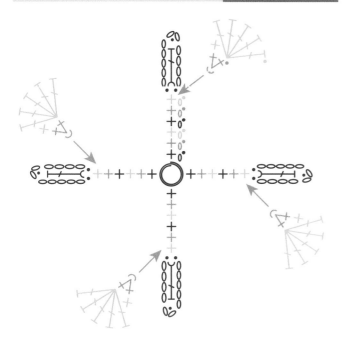

PATTERN

ROUND 1: In green, MR, ch 1, 4 sc in ring, join with sl st.

ROUND 2: Ch 1, 1 sc in each sc, join with sl st, fasten off.

ROUND 3: Join pink, ch 1, 1 sc in each sc, join with sl st.

ROUND 4: Rep round 3.

ROUND 5: Rep round 3.

ROUND 6: Rep round 3.

ROUND 7: * (Ch 4, 1 dc, ch 2 picot, ch 5, sl st) in blo of next sc, sl st in next sc; rep from * 3 times more, fasten off.

ROUND 8: Join purple to flo of any sc from round 6, (2 sc in flo of sc) 4 times, join with sl st.

ROUND 9: (4 dc in next sc, 1 sc in foll sc) 4 times, join with sl st. Fasten off, weave in ends.

Take 2 strands of pink, fold them in half and secure inside center of the flower, tie knots in the ends and trim.

⬭ MR - magic ring   **● sl st -** slip stitch   **dc -** double crochet   **dc in back loop**

⬭ ch - chain   **+ sc -** single crochet

ch 2 picot   **sc in front loop**

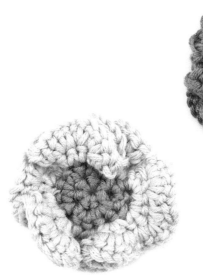

FLOWER 20 — Hyperbolic Flower

Repeat

PATTERN

ROUND 1: In color A, MR, ch 1, 8 sc in ring, join with sl st.

ROUND 2: Ch 1, (2 sc in each sc) 8 times, join with sl st, fasten off.

ROUND 3: Join color B, ch 1, (3 sc in each sc) 16 times, join with sl st.

ROUND 4: Ch 1, (3 sc in each sc) 48 times, join with sl st.

Fasten off, weave in ends.

⬭ MR - magic ring

⬭ ch - chain

● sl st - slip stitch

+ sc - single crochet

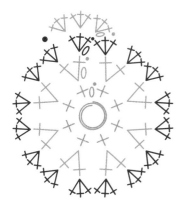

FLOWER 21

Hyperbolic Flower Version 2

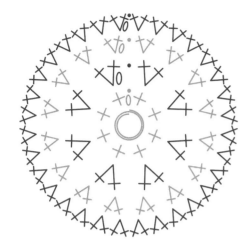

PATTERN

ROUND 1: MR, ch 1, 8 sc in ring, join with sl st.

ROUND 2: Ch 1, * 2 sc in each sc; rep from * to end, join with sl st.

ROUND 3: Rep round 2 until flower is desired size.

Fasten off, weave in ends.

Tip: Use a hook 1/2-1 size smaller than your yarn recommends.

⭘ MR - magic ring

⬭ ch - chain

• sl st - slip stitch

+ sc - single crochet

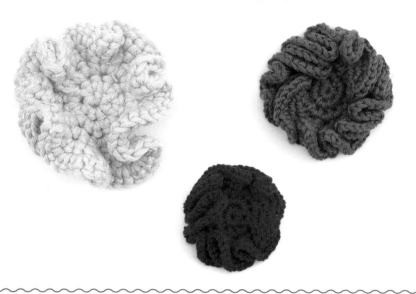

FLOWER 22

Lacy Corsage Flower

⬭ ch - chain

+ sc - single crochet

⊺ dc - double crochet

PATTERN

ROW 1: Ch 25, make first sc in 2nd ch from hook, 1 sc in each ch to end, turn.

ROW 2: Ch 1, 1 sc in sc, (ch 3, 1 sc in sc) to end, turn.

ROW 3: In ch-3 sp work ch 4 (counts as 1 dc, ch-1), 1 dc, (ch 1, 1 dc) 3 times, * in next ch-3 sp work 1 dc, (ch 1, 1 dc) 4 times; rep from * to end.

ROW 4: Fasten off leaving a long tail to sew up.

Roll in flower shape, sewing to secure in place as you roll.
To vary the size of the flower, make the starting chain longer.

FLOWER 23 — Large Center, Small Petals Flower

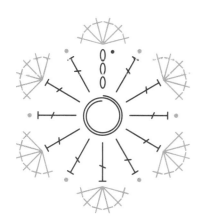

PATTERN

ROUND 1: In color A, MR, ch 3, 12 dc in ring, join with sl st.

ROUND 2: Join color B, (6 sc in next dc, sl st in foll dc) 6 times.
Fasten off, weave in ends.

MR - magic ring
ch - chain
sl st - slip stitch

+ sc - single crochet
dc - double crochet

FLOWER 24 — Daffodil Large

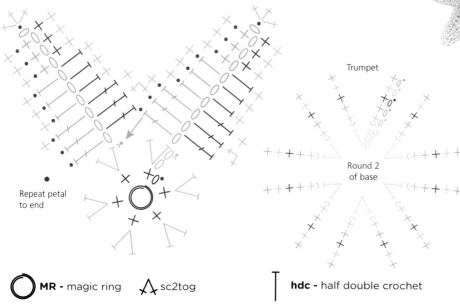

Trumpet

Round 2
of base

MR - magic ring
ch - chain
sl st - slip stitch
sl st in back loop

△ sc2tog
+ sc - single crochet
‡ sc in front loop

hdc - half double crochet
dc - double crochet

Repeat petal to end

PATTERN

Base and petal

ROUND 1: MR, ch 1, 6 sc in ring, join with sl st.

ROUND 2: Ch 2, (2 hdc in each sc) 6 times, join with sl st in blo.

ROUND 3: * Ch 10, work first sc in 2nd ch from hook, 1 sc in each of next 2 ch, 1 hdc in each of next 3 ch, 1 dc in each of next 3 ch to bottom, skip 1 st in round, sl st in blo of next st; rep from * 5 times more.

ROUND 4: * working up opposite side of foundation ch, 1 dc in each of next 3 ch, 1 hdc in each of next 3 ch, 1 sc in each of next 3 ch, sl st in each of next 10 sts of round 3 down petal; rep from * 5 times more.

ROUND 5: * Sc2tog, 1 sc in each of next 7 sts, 3 sc in next st (turning the corner at the point of the petal), 1 sc in each of next 7 sts, sc2tog; rep from * 5 times more.
Fasten off, weave in ends.

Trumpet

ROUND 1: Join yarn in flo of round 2 of base, ch 1, * 1 sc in each flo, rep from * 11 times, join with sl st.

ROUND 2: Ch 1, * 1 sc in each sc; rep from * to end, join with sl st.

ROUND 3: Rep the last round 3 times more.
Fasten off, weave in ends.

FLOWER 25 — Large Flower Motif

PATTERN

Base Round: In color A, ch 6, join with sl st to make a ring.

ROUND 1: Ch 1, 8 sc in ring, join with sl st.

ROUND 2: Join color B, ch 4, 1 tr in same st, ch 3, * 2 tr, ch 3; rep from * in each sc, join with sl st in top of ch-4

ROUND 3: Sl st in next ch-3 sp, (ch 3, 2 dc, ch 3, 3 dc, ch 1) in same ch-3 sp, * (3 dc, ch 3, 3 dc, ch 1) all in next ch-3 sp; rep from * 6 times more, join with sl st in top of first ch-3.

ROUND 4: (9 dc in next ch-3 sp, 1 sc in ch-1 sp) 8 times, join with sl st. Fasten off, weave in ends.

- ⬭ **ch -** chain
- ● **sl st -** slip stitch
- ✛ **sc -** single crochet
- ⊤ **dc -** double crochet
- ⧧ **tr -** treble crochet

FLOWER 26 — Lacy Ruffle Circular Flower

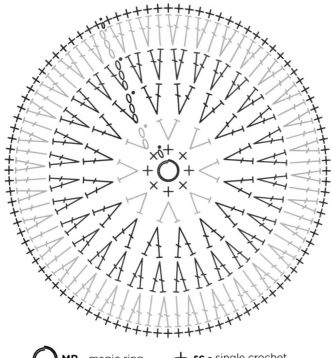

PATTERN

ROUND 1: In stem color, MR, ch 1, 8 sc in ring, join with sl st.

ROUND 2: Ch 2, hdc in same st,* 2 hdc in each sc; rep from * to end, join with sl st.

ROUND 3: Ch 3, dc in same st,* 2 dc in each hdc; rep from * to end, join with sl st, fasten off leaving a long length for sewing up.

ROUND 4: Join flower color, ch 3, dc in same st, * 2 dc in each dc; rep from * to end, join with sl st.

ROUND 5: Ch 3, * 2 dc in next st, 1 dc in next st; rep from * to end, join with sl st, fasten off and weave in ends.

ROUND 6: Join edge color, ch 1 * 1 sc in each dc; rep from * to end, join with sl st.
Fasten off.

Pinch in a rough cone and sew in place at end of round 3.
Wrap the yarn around the green section to make a stem.

- ◯ **MR -** magic ring
- ⬭ **ch -** chain
- ● **sl st -** slip stitch
- ✛ **sc -** single crochet
- **hdc -** half double crochet
- **dc -** double crochet

FLOWER 27 — Large Star and Round Flower Motif

PATTERN

ROUND 1: In color A, MR, ch 1, 6 sc in ring, join with sl st, fasten off.

ROUND 2: Join color B to any sc, ch 3, 2-dc bobble, ch 3, * 3-dc bobble, ch 3; rep from * 5 times more, join with sl st in top of ch-3, fasten off.

ROUND 3: Rejoin color A to top of any 3-dc bobble, ch 1, 1 sc in same st, 6 dc in ch-3 sp, * 1 sc in top of next 3-dc bobble, 6 dc in ch-3 sp; rep from * 5 times more, join with sl st to ch-1, fasten off.

ROUND 4: Rejoin color B in any sc, (ch 3, 2-dc bobble, ch 3, 3-dc bobble) all in sc, ch 3, * (3-dc bobble, ch 3, 3-dc bobble) all in next sc, ch 3; rep from * 4 times more, join with sl st in top of ch-3, fasten off.

ROUND 5: Rejoin color A to top of any 3-dc bobble, ch 1, sc in same st, 6 dc in ch-3 sp, * 1 sc in top of 3-dc bobble, 6 dc in next ch-3 sp; rep from * 10 times more, join with sl st in ch-1.
Fasten off, weave in ends.

⭕ **MR** - magic ring	✛ **sc** - single crochet	⬮ 3-dc bobble
⬯ **ch** - chain	**dc** - double crochet	
• **sl st** - slip stitch		

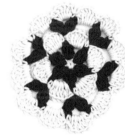

FLOWER 28 — Leaf

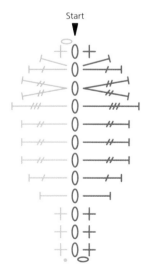

Work in rows up both sides of a single chain

PATTERN

ROW 1: Ch 13, work 1 sc in 2nd ch from hook, 1 sc in each of next 2 sts, 1 hdc in next ch, 1 dc in foll ch, 1 tr in each of next 3 ch, 1 dtr in next ch, 2 tr in foll ch, (1 dc, 1 hdc) in next ch, 1 sc in end ch.

ROW 2: Working along the opposite side of ch, ch 1, 1 sc in next ch, (1 hdc, 1 dc) in next ch, 2 tr in foll ch, 1 dtr in next ch, 1 tr in each of next 3 ch, 1 dc in foll ch, 1 hdc in next ch, 1 sc in each of next 3 ch, sl st in end.
Fasten off, weave in ends.

⬯ **ch** - chain	**dc** - double crochet
• **sl st** - slip stitch	
✛ **sc** - single crochet	**tr** - treble crochet · **dtr** - double treble crochet
hdc - half double crochet	

FLOWER 29 — Water Lily Pad

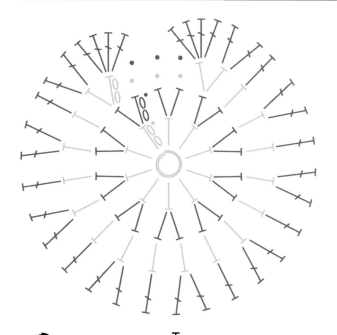

MR - magic ring

ch - chain

sl st - slip stitch

hdc - half double crochet

dc - double crochet

PATTERN

ROUND 1: MR, ch 2, 10 hdc in ring, join with sl st.

ROUND 2: Ch 2, * 2 hdc in each hdc; rep from * to end, join with sl st.

ROUND 3: Ch 2, 2 hdc in next st, 1 hdc in each of next 15 sts, 2 hdc in next st, sl st in each of next 3 sts.

ROUND 4: 4 dc in next st, 2 dc in foll st, (1 dc in next st, 2 dc in foll st) 8 times, 4 dc in next st, sl st in each of next 3 sts. Fasten off, weave in ends.

FLOWER 30 — Medium Pointed Petal Flower

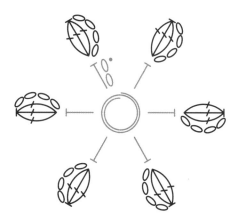

MR - magic ring

ch - chain

sl st - slip stitch

hdc - half double crochet

 3-dc bobble

PATTERN

ROUND 1: In color A, MR, ch 2, 6 hdc in ring, join with sl st, fasten off.

ROUND 2: Join color B in any st, (ch 4, 3-dc bobble, fasten off and weave in ends) in each hdc.

FLOWER 31 — Morning Glory

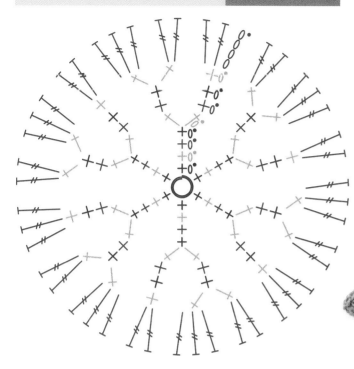

PATTERN

ROUND 1: In white, MR, ch 1, 6 sc in ring, join with sl st.

ROUND 2: Ch 1, * 1 sc in each sc; rep from * to end, join with sl st.

ROUND 3: Rep round 2.

ROUND 4: Rep round 2.

ROUND 5: Ch 1, *2 sc in each sc; rep from * to end, join with sl st.

ROUND 6: Rep round 2.

ROUND 7: Rep round 2.

ROUND 8: Ch 1, 1 sc in same sc, 2 sc in foll sc, * 1 sc in next sc, 2 sc in foll sc; rep from * to end, join with sl st, fasten off.

ROUND 9: Join color in any st, ch 4, 2 tr in same sc, 2 tr in foll sc, * 3 tr in next sc, 2 tr in foll sc; rep from * to end.

Fasten off, weave in ends.

MR - magic ring
sl st - slip stitch
ch - chain
sc - single crochet
tr - treble crochet

FLOWER 32 — Multi Colored Layered Flower

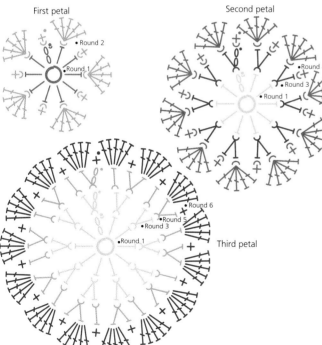

PATTERN

ROUND 1: In color A, MR, ch 2, 9 hdc in ring, join with sl st in flo.

ROUND 2: 1 sc in flo of same st as sl st, 5 dc in flo of next hdc, * 1 sc in flo of next hdc, 5 dc in flo foll hdc; rep from * to end, join with sl st in first sc, fasten off.

ROUND 3: Join color B in blo of any st in round 1, (ch 2, 1 hdc) in blo of hdc, (2 hdc in blo of next hdc) 9 times, join with sl st in ch-2.

ROUND 4: Rep round 2, fasten off.

ROUND 5: Join color C in blo of any st in round 3, (ch 2, 1 hdc) in blo of hdc, 1 hdc in blo of hdc, (2 hdc in blo of next hdc, 1 hdc in blo of foll hdc) 9 times, join with sl st in top of ch-2.

ROUND 6: 1 sc in of same st, 5 dc in of next hdc, * 1 sc in of next hdc, 5 dc in foll hdc; rep from * to end, join with sl st in first sc.

Fasten off, weave in ends.

MR - magic ring
sl st in front loop
hdc - half double crochet
ch - chain
sc - single crochet
sl st - slip stitch
sc in front loop
hdc in back loop
dc - double crochet
dc in front loop

25

FLOWER 33 — Water Lily Pad

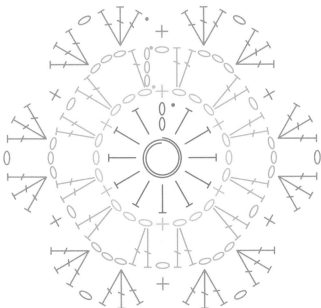

PATTERN

ROUND 1: MR, ch 2, 11 hdc in ring, join with sl st in ch-2.

ROUND 2: (Ch 3, skip 1 st, 1 sc in next hdc) 6 times, join with sl st.

ROUND 3: Sl st in ch-3 sp, (ch 3, 1 dc, ch 3, 2 dc, ch 1) in ch-3 sp, * (2 dc, ch 3, 2 dc) in next ch-3 sp, ch 1; rep from * 4 times more, join with sl st in ch-3.

ROUND 4: * (3 dc, ch 1, 3 dc) in ch-3 sp, 1 sc in ch-1 sp; rep from * 5 times more, join with sl st.

Fasten off, weave in ends.

Variation – change the color of the center by working round 1 in a different color.

MR - magic ring	**hdc -** half double crochet
ch - chain	
sl st - slip stitch	**dc -** double crochet
sc - single crochet	

FLOWER 34 — Multi Layered Flower

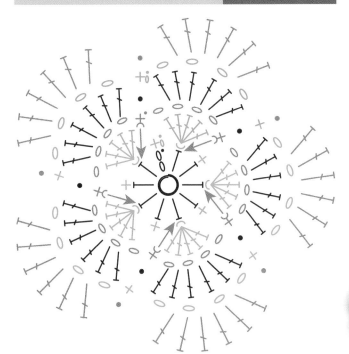

PATTERN

ROUND 1: MR, ch 2, 9 hdc in ring, join with sl st.

ROUND 2: Ch 1, 1 sc in same st, 5 dc in flo of next hdc, (1 sc in next hdc, 5 dc in flo of next hdc) 4 times, join with sl st in ch-1.

ROUND 3: Sl st in blo of next hdc of round 1 (behind petals just worked), 1 sc in same blo of hdc, ch 4, (1 sc in blo of next hdc, ch 4) 4 times, join with sl st in first sc.

ROUND 4: (6 dc in ch-4 sp, sl st in sc) 5 times.

ROUND 5: Ch 1, 1 sc in same st, ch 4, (1 sc in sl st, ch 4) 4 times, join with sl st in ch-1.

ROUND 6: (6 dc in ch-4 sp, sl st in sc) 5 times.

Fasten off, weave in ends.

MR - magic ring	**sl st -** slip stitch	sc in back loop
ch - chain	**sc -** single crochet	**hdc -** half double crochet
	dc - double crochet	dc in front loop

FLOWER 35 — Outline Leaf

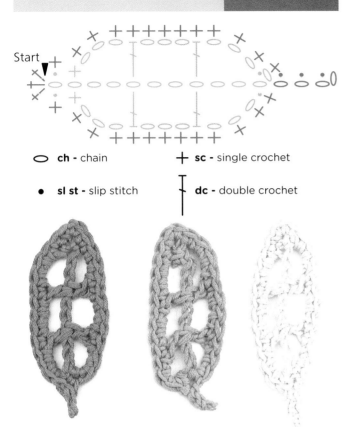

○ **ch** - chain
● **sl st** - slip stitch
＋ **sc** - single crochet
╪ **dc** - double crochet

Work in rounds around a central chain

PATTERN

ROUND 1: Ch 12, make sl st in 2nd ch from hook, (ch 3, skip 2-ch, 1 dc in next ch) twice, ch 3, skip 2-ch, 1 sc in next ch, sl st in last ch

ROUND 2: Work along the opposite side of ch as folls: sl st in first ch, 1 sc in next ch, (ch 3, skip 2-ch, 1 dc in next ch) twice, ch 3, skip 2-ch, sl st in last ch, ch 4 for stem.

ROUND 3: Make sl st in 2nd ch from hook, sl st in each of next 2 ch, 1 sc in next st, (work 3 sc in ch-3 sp, 1 sc in top of dc) twice, 3 sc in ch-3 sp, 1 sc in next st, 3 sc in next st (to make point), 1 sc in next st, (3 sc in ch-3 sp, 1 sc in top of dc) twice, 3 sc in ch-3 sp, 1 sc in next st. Fasten off, weave in ends.

FLOWER 36 — Outline Leaf Version 2

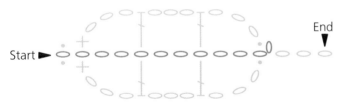

○ **ch** - chain
● **sl st** - slip stitch
＋ **sc** - single crochet
╪ **dc** - double crochet

Work in rows around a central chain

PATTERN

ROW 1: Ch 12, make sl st in 2nd ch from hook, (ch 3, skip 2-ch, 1 dc in next ch) twice, ch 3, skip 2-ch, 1 sc in next ch, sl st in last ch.

ROW 2: Work along the opposite side of ch as folls: sl st in first ch, 1 sc in next ch, (ch 3, skip 2-ch, 1 dc in next ch) twice, ch 3, skip 2-ch, sl st in last ch, ch 3 for stem. Fasten off, weave in ends.

FLOWER 37 Pansy

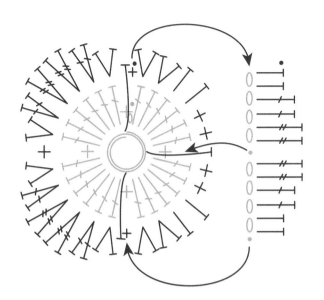

PATTERN

ROUND 1: In center color, MR, ch 1, (1 sc, 6 dc) 4 times in ring, join with sl st in top of first sc, fasten off.

ROUND 2: Join outer color to sc, long hdc in ring, * 2 hdc in next st, 2 dc in next st, 2 tr in each of next 2 sts, 2 dc in next st, 2 hdc in foll st *, 1 sc in sc; rep from * to * in next 6 sts, long hdc in ring, 1 sc in sc, 2 hdc in each of next 2 sts, 1 hdc in each of next 2 sts, 1 sc in each of next 2 sts, long hdc in ring, 1 sc in each of next 2 sts, 1 hdc in each of next 2 sts, 2 hdc in each of next 2 sts, join with sl st in long hdc.

ROUND 3: Working behind petals, ch 4, sl st in back of last long hdc from last round, ch 4, sl st in sc from last round.

ROUND 4: Work (2 hdc, 2 dc, 2 tr) all in ch-4 sp just made, then work (2 tr, 2 dc, 2 hdc) all in other ch-4 sp.
Fasten off, weave in ends.

MR - magic ring
ch - chain
sl st - slip stitch
sc - single crochet
long hdc
hdc - half double crochet
dc - double crochet
tr - treble crochet

FLOWER 38 Peony

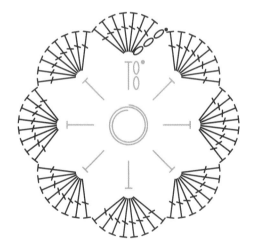

PATTERN

ROUND 1: In center color, MR, ch 2, 8 hdc in ring, join with sl st, fasten off.

ROUND 2: Join petal color, ch 3, 7 dc in hdc, * 8 dc in next hdc; rep from * 6 times more, join with sl st in ch-3.
Fasten off, weave in ends.

MR - magic ring
ch - chain
sl st - slip stitch
hdc - half double crochet
dc - double crochet

FLOWER 39 — Picot Edged Motif

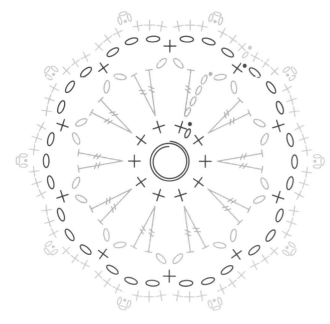

PATTERN

ROUND 1: In color A, MR, ch 1, 10 sc in ring, join with sl st, fasten off.

ROUND 2: Join color B, ch 4, tr in same st, ch 2, (2 tr in next sc, ch 2) 9 times, join with sl st, fasten off.

ROUND 3: Rejoin color A, (1 sc in ch-2 sp, ch 3) 10 times, join with sl st.

ROUND 4: ((3 sc, ch 3 picot, 3 sc) all in ch-3 sp) 10 times, join with sl st Fasten off, weave in ends.

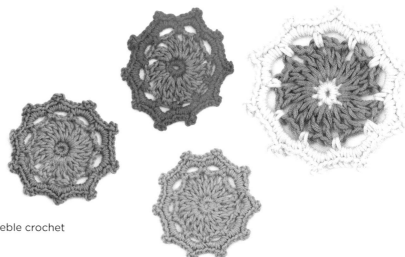

⊙ **MR -** magic ring

⬭ **ch -** chain

⊙⊙⊙ **ch 3 picot**

● **sl st -** slip stitch

+ **sc -** single crochet

tr - treble crochet

FLOWER 40 — Pointed Petal Motif Squared

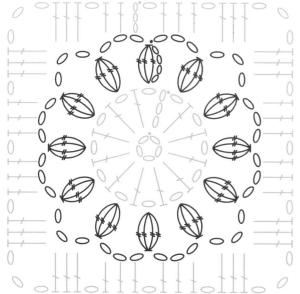

PATTERN

Base Round: Ch 5, join with sl st to make a ring.

ROUND 1: Ch 4 (counts as 1 dc and ch-1), (1 dc, ch 1) 11 times, join with sl st in 3rd ch of ch 4.

ROUND 2: Sl st in ch-1 sp, ch 4 work 3-tr bobble in same sp, ch 3, (4-tr bobble in next ch-1 sp, ch 3) 11 times, join with sl st in top of ch-4.

ROUND 3: Sl st in ch-3 sp, (ch 3, 2 dc, ch 1) in ch-3 sp, * (3 dc, ch 3, 3 dc) in ch-3 sp (corner made), ch 1, (3 dc, ch 1) in each of next two ch-3 sps; rep from * twice more, (3 dc, ch 3, 3 dc) in next ch-3 sp, (3 dc, ch 1) in last ch-3 sp, join with sl st in top of ch-3.

Fasten off, weave in ends.

⬭ **ch -** chain

● **sl st -** slip stitch

dc - double crochet

4 tr-bobble

FLOWER 41 — Poinsettia

- ⬭ **MR -** magic ring
- ⬯ **ch -** chain
- ● **sl st -** slip stitch
- ⬯⬮ **ch 2 picot**
- ⊥ **sc in back loop**
- | **hdc -** half double crochet
- ⬙ **2 tr-bobble**
- ⬙ **2 tr-bobble in front loop**

PATTERN

ROUND 1: In yellow, MR, ch 2, 5 hdc in ring, join with sl st, fasten off.

ROUND 2: Join red in blo of any st, (1 sc in blo, ch 3) 6 times, join with sl st in sc.

ROUND 3: (Sl st in next ch-3 sp, ch 4, 2-tr bobble, ch 2 picot, ch 5, sl st in same ch-3 sp) 6 times.

ROUND 4: (Sl st in flo of next hdc from round 1, ch 4, 2-tr bobble, ch 2 picot, ch 5, sl st in same flo of hdc) 6 times.
Fasten off, weave in ends.

FLOWER 42 — Popcorn Flower Motif

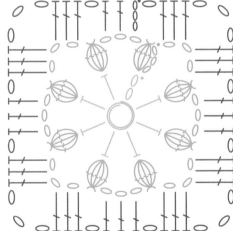

- ⬭ **MR -** magic ring
- ⬯ **ch -** chain
- ● **sl st -** slip stitch
- | **hdc -** half double crochet
- | **dc -** double crochet
- **pc -** popcorn stitch

PATTERN

ROUND 1: In center color, MR, ch 2, 7 hdc in ring, join with sl st, fasten off.

ROUND 2: Join petal color in any st, ch 3, (PC, ch 3) 8 times, join with sl st in ch-3, fasten off.

ROUND 3: Join outer color in any ch-3 sp, (ch 3 (counts as 1-dc), 2 dc, ch 1) in ch-3 sp, * (3 dc, ch 3, 3 dc, ch 1) in next ch-3 sp (corner made), (3 dc, ch 1) in foll ch-3 sp; rep from * twice more, (3 dc, ch 3, 3 dc, ch 1) in next ch-3 sp, join with sl st in top of first ch-3.
Fasten off, weave in ends.

These cute little squares would be ideal to join together to make in a larger project. I think they would look lovely as a cushion cover.

FLOWER 43 — Popcorn Flower

MR - magic ring

ch - chain

sl st - slip stitch

hdc - half double crochet

pc - popcorn stitch

PATTERN

ROUND 1: In center color, MR, ch 2, 7 hdc in ring, join with sl st, fasten off.

ROUND 2: Join petal color in any st, ch 3, (PC, ch 3) 8 times, join with sl st in ch 3.

Fasten off, weave in ends.

FLOWER 44 — Poppy

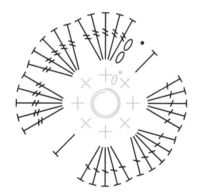

MR - magic ring

ch - chain

sl st - slip stitch

sc - single crochet

hdc - half double crochet

dc - double crochet

tr - treble crochet

PATTERN

ROUND 1: In brown, MR, ch 1, 8 sc in ring, join with sl st, fasten off.

ROUND 2: Join red in any st, ch 2, 5 tr in each of next 3 sts, 1 hdc in foll st, 5 dc in each of next 3 sts, 1 hdc in foll st, join with a sl st in ch-2.

Fasten off, weave in ends.

FLOWER 45 — Primula

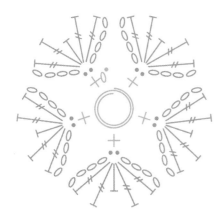

PATTERN

ROUND 1: In center color, MR, ch 1, 5 sc in ring, join with sl st, fasten off.

ROUND 2: Join petal color in any st, * sl st in next st, (ch 4, 2 tr, 1 hdc, 2 tr, ch 4, sl st) all in same st; rep from * 4 times more. Fasten off, weave in ends.

MR - magic ring	**hdc -** half double crochet
ch - chain	
sl st - slip stitch	**tr -** treble crochet
sc - single crochet	

FLOWER 46 — Round Petal Upright Flower With Leaves

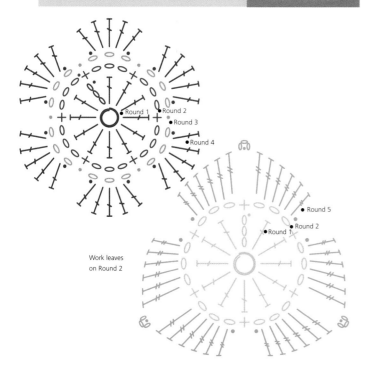

Round 1
Round 2
Round 3
Round 4

Round 5
Round 2
Round 1

Work leaves on Round 2

PATTERN

ROUND 1: In flower color, MR, ch 3, 11 dc in ring, join with sl st.

ROUND 2: (Ch 3, skip 1 st, 1 sc in next st) 6 times, join with sl st.

ROUND 3: (Ch 3, skip ch-3 sp, sl st in sc) 6 times.

ROUND 4: ((Sl st in next ch-3 sp, 5 dc, sl st) all in ch-3 sp) 6 times, fasten off.

ROUND 5: Join leaf color with sl st in ch-3 sp of round 2, * 6 tr, ch 3 picot, (6 tr, sl st) in next ch-3 sp, sl st in next ch-3 sp; rep from * twice more. Fasten off, weave in ends.

MR - magic ring	**ch 3 picot**	**sc -** single crochet	**tr -** treble crochet
ch - chain	**sl st -** slip stitch	**dc -** double crochet	

FLOWER 47 — Round Petal Upright Flower

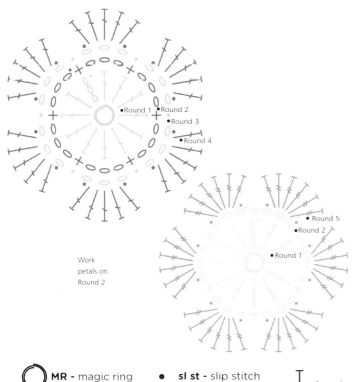

Work petals on Round 2

PATTERN

ROUND 1: MR, ch 3, 11 dc in ring, join with sl st.

ROUND 2: (Ch 3, skip 1 st, 1 sc in next st) 6 times, join with sl st.

ROUND 3: (Ch 3, skip ch-3 sp, sl st in sc) 6 times.

ROUND 4: ((Sl st in next ch-3 sp, 5 dc, sl st) all in ch-3 sp) 6 times.

ROUND 5: Sl st in ch-3 sp of round 2, * 6 tr, sl st, all in ch-3 sp, sl st in next ch-3 sp; rep from * 5 times more.

Fasten off, weave in ends.

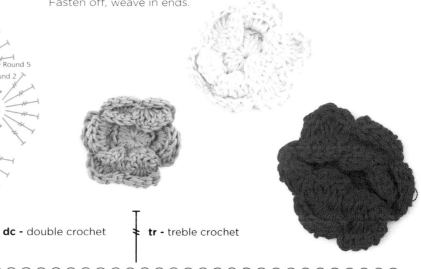

◯ **MR -** magic ring   ● **sl st -** slip stitch | **dc -** double crochet   ǂ **tr -** treble crochet

◯ **ch -** chain   + **sc -** single crochet

FLOWER 48 — Simple Chain and Flower

PATTERN

Base Round: Ch 6, join with sl st to make a ring.

ROUND 1: Ch 1, (1 sc in ring, ch 6) 5 times, join with sl st in first sc.

ROUND 2: Work 7 sc in each ch-6 sp of last round, join with sl st in first sc.

Fasten off, weave in ends.

◯ **ch -** chain

● **sl st -** slip stitch

+ **sc -** single crochet

FLOWER 49 — Simple Lily

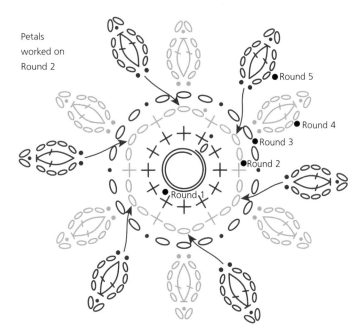

Petals worked on Round 2

Round 5
Round 4
Round 3
Round 2
Round 1

PATTERN

ROUND 1: MR, ch 1, 12 sc in ring, join with sl st.

ROUND 2: (Ch 3, skip 1 st, 1 sc in next st) 6 times, join with sl st.

ROUND 3: (Ch 3, skip ch-3 sp, sl st in sc) 6 times.

ROUND 4: Sl st in ch-3 sp from last round, * (ch 4, 2-dc bobble, ch 2 picot, ch 4, sl st) all in ch-3 sp, sl st in next ch-3 sp; rep from * 5 times more.

ROUND 5: Sl st in ch-3 sp from round 2, rep last round working in each ch-3 sp.

Fasten off, weave in ends.

- ⭕ **MR -** magic ring
- ◯ **ch -** chain
- • **sl st -** slip stitch
- ✕ **sc -** single crochet
- 👁 **ch 2 picot**
- ◇ **2 dc-bobble**

FLOWER 50 — Simplified Pansy

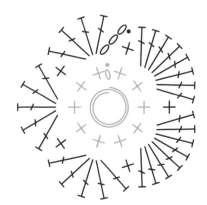

PATTERN

ROUND 1: In yellow, MR, ch 1, 10 sc in ring, join with sl st, fasten off.

ROUND 2: Join purple, ch 3, 4 dc in same st, (1 sc in next st, 5 dc in foll st) twice, (1 sc in next st, 8 dc in foll st) twice, 1 sc in last st, join with sl st.

Fasten off, weave in ends.

- ⭕ **MR -** magic ring
- ◯ **ch -** chain
- • **sl st -** slip stitch
- ✕ **sc -** single crochet
- ┼ **dc -** double crochet

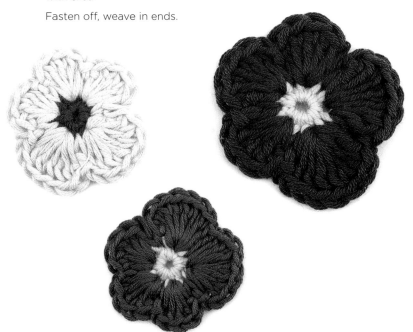

FLOWER 51 — Small Heart Shaped Leaf

PATTERN

ROUND 1: MR, ch 1, 8 sc in ring, join with sl st.

ROUND 2: 5 dc in first sc, 2 hdc in each of next 2-sc, (1 sc, ch 2 picot, 1 sc) in next sc, 2 hdc in each of next 2-sc, 5 dc in last sc, join with sl st in top of ch-1.

Fasten off, weave in ends.

MR - magic ring

ch - chain

ch 2 picot

sl st - slip stitch

sc - single crochet

hdc - half double crochet

dc - double crochet

FLOWER 52 — Square Petal Flower

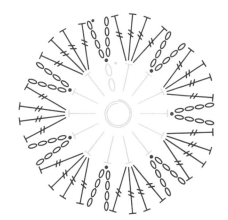

PATTERN

ROUND 1: In color A, MR, ch 2, 13 hdc in ring, join with sl st, fasten off.

ROUND 2: Join color B, (ch 4, 4 tr in next hdc, ch 4, sl st in next hdc) 7 times.

Fasten off, weave in ends.

MR - magic ring

ch - chain

sl st - slip stitch

hdc - half double crochet

tr - treble crochet

FLOWER 53 — Star Flower

PATTERN

ROUND 1: Holding 1 strand of yellow and 1 strand of pale green together, MR, ch 1, 10 sc in ring, join with sl st, fasten off.

ROUND 2: Join main petal color, 1 sc in same st, 5 dc in next st, (1 sc in next st, 5 dc in foll st) 4 times, join with sl st in first sc, fasten off.

ROUND 3: (Join highlight color in 2nd dc of petal, 1 sc in same st, 2 sc in next st, 1 sc in foll st, fasten off) 5 times.

ROUND 4: Join main petal color to first sc of highlight, (1 sc in sc, 2 sc in next sc, 2ch, 2 sc in next sc, 1 sc in next sc, 1 hdc in dc, 1 sc in sc, 1 hdc in dc) 5 times, join with sl st.

Fasten off, weave in ends.

◯ MR - magic ring

◯ ch - chain

• sl st - slip stitch

+ sc - single crochet

| hdc - half double crochet

| dc - double crochet

FLOWER 54 — Star Flower Motif

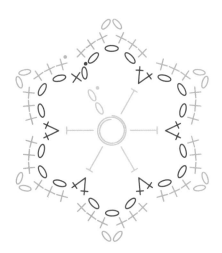

PATTERN

ROUND 1: MR, ch 2, 5 hdc in ring, join with sl st.

ROUND 2: Ch 1, 1 sc in same st, ch 3, (2 sc in next hdc, ch 3) 5 times, join with sl st.

ROUND 3: ((3 sc, ch 2, 3 sc) all in ch-3 sp) 6 times, join with sl st. Fasten off, weave in ends.

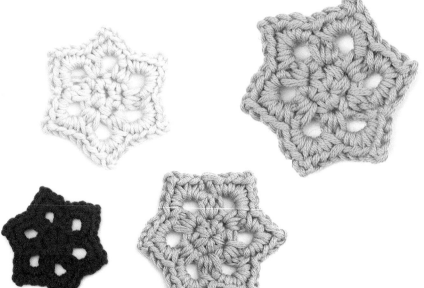

◯ MR - magic ring

◯ ch - chain

• sl st - slip stitch

+ sc - single crochet

| hdc - half double crochet

Sweet William

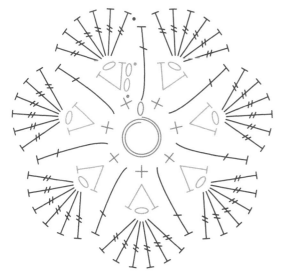

PATTERN

ROUND 1: In center color, MR, ch 1, 7 sc in ring, join with sl st.

ROUND 2: Ch 2, (1 hdc, ch 1, 1 hdc) in same sl, (1 hdc, ch 1, 1 hdc) in each of next 6 sc, join with sl st in ch 2, fasten off.

ROUND 3: Join petal color in ch-1 sp, (6 tr in ch-1 sp, long dc between scs of round 1) 7 times, join with sl st.

Fasten off, weave in ends.

○ **MR -** magic ring

○ **ch -** chain

● **sl st -** slip stitch

+ **sc -** single crochet

| **hdc -** half double crochet

⧧ **tr -** treble crochet

} long dc

Daffodil Small

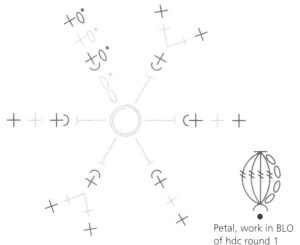

Petal, work in BLO of hdc round 1

PATTERN

Trumpet

ROUND 1: MR, ch 2, 5 hdc in ring, join with sl st.

ROUND 2: Ch 1, * 1 sc in flo of each hdc; rep from * to end, join with sl st.

ROUND 3: Ch 1, (1 sc in each of next 2 sts, 2 sc in foll st) twice, join with sl st.

ROUND 4: Ch 1, 1 sc in each sc around, join with sl st.

Fasten off, weave in ends.

Petals

ROUND 1: Join yellow in any blo of round 1 of trumpet, (ch 4, 4-tr bobble in blo of hdc, fasten off).

ROUND 2: Rep for each petal around trumpet.

Weave in ends.

○ **MR -** magic ring

○ **ch -** chain

● **sl st -** slip stitch

+ **sc -** single crochet

⊥ sc in front loop

| **hdc -** half double crochet

 4 tr- bobble

37

FLOWER 57 — Spike Flower Motif

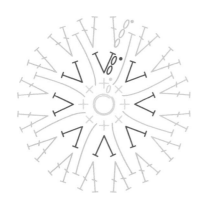

PATTERN

ROUND 1: In color A, MR, ch 1, 8 sc in ring, join with sl st, fasten off.

ROUND 2: Join color B in any sc, ch 2, 2 hdc in same st, (2 hdc in each sc) 7 times, join with sl st in ch 2, fasten off.

ROUND 3: Rejoin color A in any hdc, ch 3, dc in same st, 2 dc in next hdc, long hdc between scs of round 1, (2 dc in each of next 2 hdc, long hdc between scs of round 1) 7 times, join with sl st.

Fasten off, weave in ends.

MR - magic ring

ch - chain

sl st - slip stitch

sc - single crochet

hdc - half double crochet

dc - double crochet

long hdc

FLOWER 58 — Star and Round Flower Motif

PATTERN

ROUND 1: In color A, MR, ch 1, 6 sc in ring, join with sl st, fasten off.

ROUND 2: Join color B, (ch 3, 2-dc bobble) in same sc, ch 3, (3-dc bobble, ch 3) 5 times, join with sl st in first ch-3, fasten off.

ROUND 3: Rejoin color A in top of any 3-dc bobble, ch 1, 1 sc in same st, 5 dc in ch-3 sp, (1 sc in top of next 3-dc bobble, 5 dc in ch-3 sp) 5 times, join with sl st in first sc.

Fasten off, weave in ends.

MR - magic ring

ch - chain

sl st - slip stitch

sc - single crochet

 3-dc bobble

dc - double crochet

FLOWER 59

Star Flower Motif

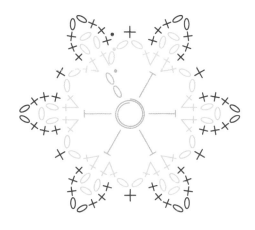

PATTERN

ROUND 1: MR, ch 2, 5 hdc in ring, join with sl st.

ROUND 2: (Ch 1, 1 sc, ch 3, 2 sc) all in same st, * ch 2, (2 sc, ch 3, 2 sc) all in next hdc; rep from * 4 times more, ch 2, join with sl st in ch-1.

ROUND 3: * (3 sc, ch 2, 3 sc) all in ch-3 sp, 1 sc in ch-2 sp; rep from * 5 times more, join with sl st.

Fasten off, weave in ends.

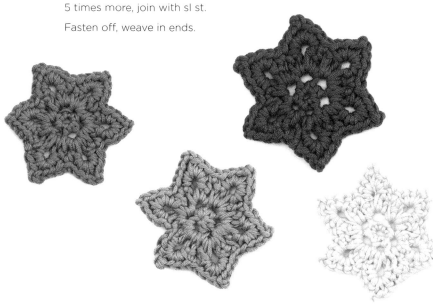

MR - magic ring

ch - chain

sl st - slip stitch

sc - single crochet

hdc - half double crochet

FLOWER 60

Sunflower

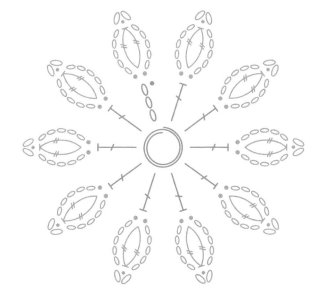

PATTERN

ROUND 1: In brown, MR, ch 3, 9 dc in ring, join with sl st, fasten off.

ROUND 2: Join yellow with sl st in any st, * (ch 5, 2-tr bobble, ch 2 picot, ch 5, sl st) all in same st, sl st in next dc; rep from * 9 times more.

Fasten off, weave in ends.

MR - magic ring

ch - chain

ch 2 picot

sl st - slip stitch

dc - double crochet

2 tr-bobble

FLOWER 61 — Sweet William Version 2

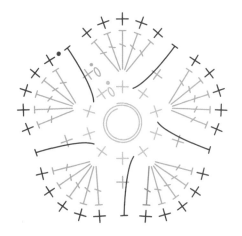

PATTERN

ROUND 1: In color A, MR, ch 1, 10 sc in ring, join with sl st, fasten off.

ROUND 2: Join color B in any st, ch 1, 1 sc in same st, 5 dc in next sc, (1 sc in next sc, 5 dc in foll sc) 4 times, join with sl st in first sc, fasten off.

ROUND 3: Rejoin color A in first dc of 5-dc petal, (sc in each of next 5-dc, long hdc between scs of round 1) 5 times, join with sl st. Fasten off, weave in ends.

MR - magic ring

ch - chain

sl st - slip stitch

sc - single crochet

dc - double crochet

long hdc

FLOWER 62 — Tudor Rose Motif

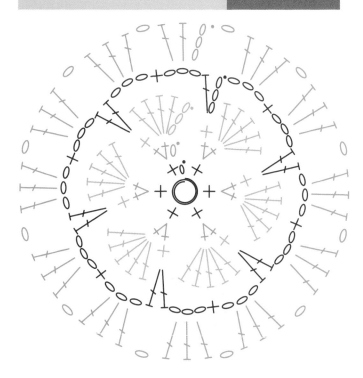

PATTERN

ROUND 1: In color A, MR, ch 1, 6 sc in ring, join with sl st.

ROUND 2: Ch 1, 2 sc in same st, 2 sc in each sc around, join with sl st, fasten off.

ROUND 3: Join color B in any sc, ch 3, 4 dc in same st, 1 sc in next sc, (5 dc in next sc, 1 sc in foll sc) 5 times, join with sl st, fasten off.

ROUND 4: Join color C to any sc, ch 3, 1 dc in same st, ch 3, skip 2 sts, 1 sc in 3rd dc of 5-dc petal, ch 3, skip 2 sts, (2 dc in sc, ch 3, skip 2 sts, 1 sc in 3rd dc of 5-dc petal, ch 3) 5 times, join with sl st in ch-3.

ROUND 5: Sl st in next ch-3 sp, (ch 3, 2 dc) in ch-3 sp, ch 1, (3 dc in ch-3 sp, ch 1) 11 times, join with sl st in ch-3.

Fasten off, weave in ends.

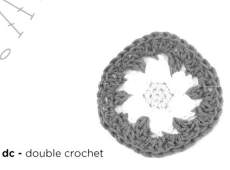

MR - magic ring

ch - chain

sl st - slip stitch

sc - single crochet

dc - double crochet

Tulip Motif

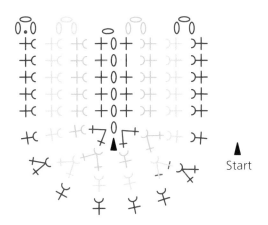

PATTERN

Rows 2-4 are worked in BLO.

ROW 1: Ch 7, make first sc in 2nd ch from hook, 1 sc in each of next 4 ch, 4 sc in last ch around end, working up opposite side of ch; 1 sc in each of next 5-ch.

ROW 2: Ch 3, turn, 1 sc in blo of same st, 1 sc in each blo of next 4-sc, (2 sc in blo of next sc, 1 sc in blo of foll sc) twice, 1 sc in each blo of next 5-sc up other side.

ROW 3: Ch 3, turn, 1 sc in same st, 1 sc in each blo of next 5-sc, 2 sc in blo of next sc, 1 sc in each blo of next 2-sc, 2 sc only in blo of foll sc, 1 sc in each blo of next 6-sc.

ROW 4: Ch 3, turn, 1 sc in blo of same st, 1 sc in each blo of next 5-sc, 2 sc in blo of next sc, 1 sc in each blo of next 4-sc, 2 sc in blo of next sc, 1 sc in each blo of next 6-sc, ch 3, sl st in same st.

Fasten off, weave in ends.

This simple tulip motif would look striking decorating a bag or even a skirt.

Add some leaves and chain for the stems and make a brightly colored tulip scene.

⬯ **ch -** chain

✛ **sc -** single crochet

⋇ sc in back loop

White Lily

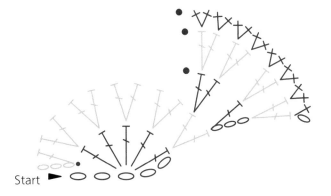

Start ▶

PATTERN

ROW 1: Ch 5, work 5 dc in 3rd ch from hook, sl st in last ch, ch 3, turn.

ROW 2: Work 1 dc in same st, 2 dc in each dc to end, ch 3, turn.

ROW 3: Rep last row.

ROW 4: Work 1 dc in same st, 2 dc in each dc to end, ch 1, turn.

ROW 5: Work 1 sc in same st, 2 sc in each dc to end.

Fasten off, weave in ends.

● Repeat to end

⬯ **ch -** chain

● **sl st -** slip stitch

✛ **sc -** single crochet

╪ **dc -** double crochet

FLOWER 65 — V Shaped Leaf

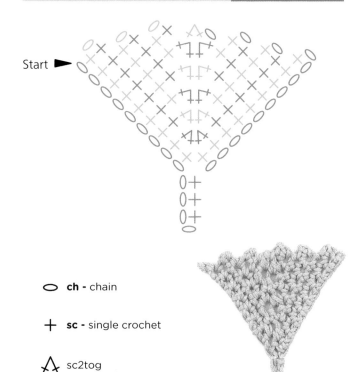

Start ►

○ **ch** - chain

✛ **sc** - single crochet

⋀ sc2tog

PATTERN

ROW 1: Ch 13, make first sc in 2nd ch from hook, 1 sc in each of next 2ch (stem made), ch 10.

ROW 2: Make 1 sc in 2nd ch from hook, 1 sc in each of next 8-ch, skip stem, 1 sc in each of next 9-ch, ch 1, turn.

ROW 3: 1 sc in each of next 7-sc, (sc2tog) twice, 1 sc in each of next 6-sc, ch 1, turn.

ROW 4: 1 sc in each of next 5-sc, (sc2tog) twice, 1 sc in each of next 5-sc, ch 1, turn.

ROW 5: 1 sc in each of next 4-sc, (sc2tog) twice, 1 sc in each of next 3-sc, ch 1, turn.

ROW 6: 1 sc in each of next 2-sc, (sc2tog) twice, 1 sc in each of next 2-sc, ch 1, turn.

ROW 7: 1 sc in next sc, (sc2tog) twice, ch 1, turn.

ROW 8: Sc2tog.

Fasten off, weave in ends.

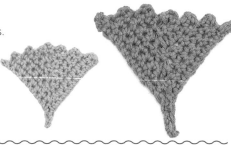

FLOWER 66 — Water Lily Flower

PATTERN

ROUND 1: MR, ch 1, 6 sc in ring, join with sl st.

ROUND 2: Ch 1, 1 sc in same st, ch 2, (1 sc in sc, ch 2) 5 times, join with sl st.

ROUND 3: Ch 1, 1 sc in same st, (ch 2, 1 sc, ch 2) all in ch-2 sp, * 1 sc in sc, (ch 2, 1 sc, ch 2) all in ch-2 sp; rep from * 5 times more, join with sl st.

ROUND 4: * (Ch 5, 3- tr bobble, ch 2 picot, ch 5, sl st) all in ch-2 sp of round 3, sl st in next ch-2 sp; rep from * 11 times more, sl st in ch-2 sp of round 2.

ROUND 5: * (Ch 5, 3-tr bobble, ch 2 picot, ch 5, sl st) all in ch-2 sp of round 2, sl st in next ch-2 sp of round 2; rep from * 5 times more.

Fasten off, weave in ends.

 **MR** - magic ring

○ **ch** - chain

 ch 2 picot

● **sl st** - slip stitch

 3 tr-bobble

✛ **sc** - single crochet

42

MOTIF 1

PATTERN

Base Round: Using Color A, ch 4; join with sl st to first ch to form a ring.

ROUND 1: (Right Side) Ch 1 (NOT counted as first st), 8 sc in ring; join with sl st to first sc. (8 sc).

ROUND 2: Ch 3 (counts as first dc, now and throughout), [yo, insert hook in same st as joining, pull up lp, yo, draw through 2 lps on hook] 3 times (4 lps on hook), yo, draw through all 4 lps (first 4-bob made), ch 2; [4-bob in next sc, ch 2] around; join with sl st to first dc (3rd ch of beginning ch-3). Fasten off Color A and weave in all ends. (8 bobbles & 8 ch-2 sps).

ROUND 3: With right side facing, join Color B with sl st to any first ch-2 sp, ch 3, 2 dc in same sp, ch 1, (3-bob, ch 3, 3-bob) in next ch-2 sp, ch 1, *3 dc in next ch-2 sp, ch 1, (3-bob, ch 3, 3-bob) in next ch-2 sp, ch 1; rep from * around; join with sl st to first dc. Fasten off Color B and weave in all ends. (8 bobbles, 12 dc, 8 ch-1 sps & 4 ch-3 sps).

⬭ **ch** - chain	**dc** - double crochet	**4-dc bobble**
● **sl st** - slip stitch		
+ **sc** - single crochet	3-dc bobble	first 4-dc bobble

PATTERN

Base Round: Using Color A, ch 4; join with sl st to first ch to form a ring.

ROUND 1: (Right Side) Ch 3 (counts as first dc, now and throughout), 15 dc in ring; join with sl st to first dc (3rd ch of beginning ch-3). (16 dc Fasten off Color A and weave in all ends.

ROUND 2: With right side facing, join Color B with sl st to same st as joining, ch 1 (NOT counted as first st), sc in same st, ch 1, skip next dc, 7 dc in next dc, ch 1, skip next dc, *sc in next dc, ch 1, skip next dc, 7 dc in next dc, ch 1, skip next dc; rep from * around; join with sl st to first sc. (28 dc, 4 sc & 8 ch-1 sps) Fasten off Color B and weave in all ends.

ROUND 3: With right side facing, join Color C with sl st to last ch-1 sp on Round 2, ch 3, [yo, insert hook in same st as joining, pull up lp, yo, draw through 2 lps on hook] 3 times (4 lps on hook), yo, draw through all 4 lps (first 4-bob made), ch 2, 4-bob in next ch-1 sp, ch 2, skip next 3 dc, sc in next dc (center dc of 7-dc group), ch 2, skip next 3 dc, *[4-bob in next ch-1 sp, ch 2] 2 times, sc in center dc of next 7-dc group, ch 2; rep from * around; join with sl st to first dc. (8 bobbles, 4 sc & 12 ch-2 sps) Fasten off Color C and weave in all ends.

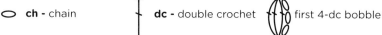

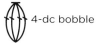

⬭ **ch** - chain

● **sl st** - slip stitch

✚ **sc** - single crochet

| **dc** - double crochet

first 4-dc bobble

4-dc bobble

MOTIF 3

PATTERN

Base Round: Using Color A, ch 4; join with sl st to first ch to form a ring.

ROUND 1: (Right Side) Ch 1 (NOT counted as first st), *sc in ring, ch 4, 4tr-bob in ring, ch 4; rep from * 3 times more; join with sl st to first sc. (4 bobbles, 4 sc & 8 ch-4 lps) Fasten off Color A and weave in all ends.

ROUND 2: With right side facing, using Color B, join with sc to 2nd ch of second ch-4 lp (after first bobble), ch 5, skip next 2 ch, skip next sc, on next ch-4 lp, skip next 2 ch, sc in next (3rd) ch, ch 3, skip next ch, skip next bobble, *on next ch-4 lp, sc in 2nd ch, ch 5, on next ch-4 lp, sc in 3rd ch, ch 3; rep from * around; join with sl st to first sc. (8 sc, 4 ch-5 lps & 4 ch 3 lps)

ROUND 3: Sl st in first ch-5 lp, ch 3 (counts as first dc), (2 dc, ch 1, 3 dc) in same lp, ch 1, 3 dc in next ch-3 lp, ch 1, *(3 dc, ch 1, 3 dc) in next ch-5 lp, ch 1, 3 dc in next ch-3 lp, ch 1; rep from * around; join with sl st to first dc (3rd ch of beg ch-3). (36 dc & 12 ch-1 sps) Fasten off Color B and weave in all ends.

- ⬭ **ch -** chain
- ● **sl st -** slip stitch
- + **sc -** single crochet
- | **dc -** double crochet
- ⨂ 4-tr bobble

48

MOTIF 4

PATTERN

Base Round: Using Color A, ch 4; join with sl st to first ch to form a ring.

ROUND 1: (Right Side) Ch 5 (counts as first dc and ch-2), [dc in ring, ch 2] 7 times; join with sl st to first dc (3rd ch of beg ch-5). (8 dc & 8 ch-2 sps).

ROUND 2: Sl st in next ch-2 sp, ch 2 (counts as first hdc), (3 dc, hdc) in same sp, *(hdc, 3 dc, hdc) in next ch-2 sp; rep from * around; join with sl st to first hdc (2nd ch of beg ch-2).

ROUND 3: Ch 8 (counts as first dc and ch-5), skip next 3 dc, dc in sp between next 2 hdc, ch 7, skip next 3 dc, *dc in sp between next 2 hdc, ch 5, skip next 3 dc, dc in sp between next 2 hdc, ch 7, skip next 3 dc; rep from * around; join with sl st to first dc (3rd ch of beg ch-8). (8 dc, 4 ch-5 lps & 4 ch-7 lps)

ROUND 4: Sl st in next ch-5 lp, ch 3 (counts as first dc), 3 dc in same lp, ch 1, (3 dc, ch 1, 3 dc) in next ch-7 lp, ch 1, *4 dc in next ch-5 lp, ch 1, (3 dc, ch 1, 3 dc) in next ch-7 lp, ch 1; rep from * around; join with sl st to first dc (3rd ch of beg ch-3). (40 dc & 12 ch-1 sps)

Fasten off and weave in all ends.

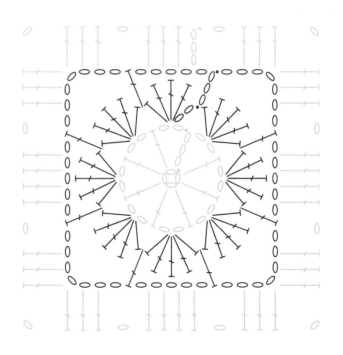

○ **ch -** chain

● **sl st -** slip stitch

hdc - half double crochet

dc - double crochet

MOTIF 5

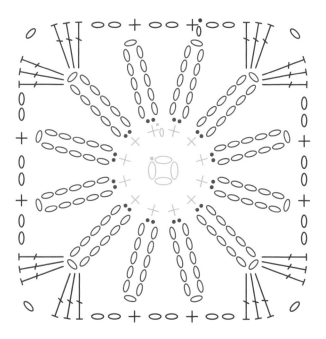

PATTERN

Base Round: Using Color A, ch 4; join with sl st to first ch to form a ring.

ROUND 1: (Right Side) Ch 1 (NOT counted as first st, now and throughout), 12 sc in ring; join with sl st to first sc. (12 sc)

ROUND 2: Ch 11, sl st in same st as joining, *(sl st, ch 11, sl st) in next sc; rep from * around. Fasten off Color A and weave in all ends.

ROUND 3: With right side facing, join Color B with sl st to any ch-11 lp (at top of petal), ch 1, sc in same lp, ch 2, sc in top of next ch-11 lp, ch 2, (3 dc, ch 1, 3 dc) in next ch-11 lp, ch 2, *[sc in top of next lp, ch 2] 2 times, (3 dc, ch 1, 3 dc) in next lp, ch 2; rep from * around; join with sl st to first sc. Fasten off Color B and weave in all ends.

○ **ch -** chain   + **sc -** single crochet

● **sl st -** slip stitch   ╪ **dc -** double crochet

PATTERN

Base Round: Using Color A, ch 4; join with sl st to first ch to form a ring.

ROUND 1: (Right Side) Ch 3 (counts as first dc), yo, insert hook in ring, pull up lp, yo, draw through 2 lps on hook (2 lps on hook), yo and draw through all lps (first 2-bob made), ch 2, [2-bob in ring, ch 2] 7 times; join with sl st to first dc (3rd ch of beg ch-3). (8 bobbles & 8 ch-2 sps).

ROUND 2: Sl st in first ch-2 sp, ch 2 (counts as first hdc), (3 dc, hdc) in same sp, *(hdc, 3 dc, hdc) in next ch-2 sp; rep from * around; join with sl st to first hdc (2nd ch of beg ch-2). (8 petals) Fasten off and weave in all ends.

ROUND 3: With right side facing, working behind petals (bend them forward out of the way), using Color A, join with sc to top of any bobble in Round 1, ch 5, sc in next bobble, ch 3, *sc in next bobble, ch 5, sc in next bobble, ch 3; rep from * around; join with sl st to first sc. (8 sc, 4 ch-3 lps & 4 ch-5 lps)

ROUND 4: Sl st in first ch-5 lp, ch 1, (NOT counted as first st), (sc, hdc, dc, ch 1, dc, hdc, sc) in same lp, ch 1, 3 sc in next ch-3 lp, ch 1, *(sc, hdc, dc, ch 1, dc, hdc, sc) in next ch-5 lp, ch 1, 3 sc in next ch-3 lp, ch 1; rep from * around; join with sl st to first sc. Fasten off and weave in all ends.

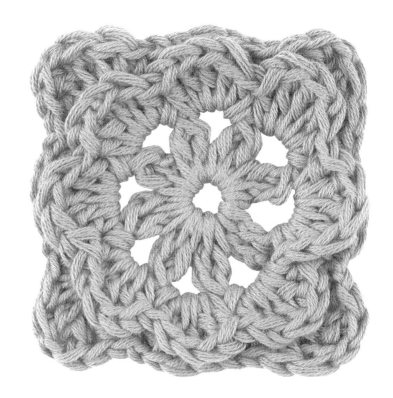

⬭ **ch** - chain		│ **hdc** - half double crochet	◇	2-dc bobble
• **sl st** - slip stitch				
+ **sc** - single crochet		│ **dc** - double crochet	◇	first 2-dc bobble

MOTIF 7

PATTERN

Base Round: Using Color A, ch 4; join with sl st to first ch to form a ring.

ROUND 1: (Right Side) Ch 4 (counts as first dc and ch-1), [dc in ring, ch 1] 11 times; join with sl st to first dc (3rd ch of beg ch-4). (12 dc & 12 ch-1 sps) Fasten off Color A and weave in all ends.

ROUND 2: With right side facing, join Color B with sl st in first ch-1 sp, ch 4 (counts as first hdc & ch-2), hdc in same sp, [(hdc, ch 2, hdc) in next ch-1 sp] around; join with sl st to first hdc (2nd ch of beg ch-4). (24 hdc & 12 ch-2 sps)

ROUND 3: Ch 1 (NOT counted as first st), sc in sp between last and first hdc (sp directly under join), 8 hdc in next ch-2 sp, *sc in sp between next 2 hdc, 8 hdc in next ch-2 sp; rep from * around; join with sl st to first sc. (12 petals & 12 sc) Fasten off Color B and weave in all ends.

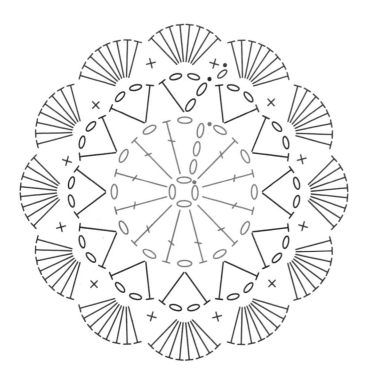

⬭ **ch** - chain	⊺	**hdc** - half double crochet
• **sl st** - slip stitch		
+ **sc** - single crochet	⊧	**dc** - double crochet

MOTIF 8

3-Double Treble Bobble (3dtr-bob): Wrap yarn three times around hook, insert hook into st or sp indicated, pull up lp (5 lps on hook), [yo, draw through 2 lps on hook] 3 times (2 lps on hook), *wrap yarn three times around hook, insert hook in same st or sp, pull up lp, [yo, draw through 2 lps on hook] 3 times, rep from * once more (4 lps on hook), yo and draw through all 4 lps.

Note: The first Bobble Stitch in a round is started differently to subsequent bobbles in round. Instructions for the first bobble are included within the pattern. For subsequent bobbles follow the instructions above.

PATTERN

Base Round: Using Color A, ch 4; join with sl st to first ch to form a ring.

ROUND 1: (Right Side) Ch 1 (NOT counted as first st), 8 sc in ring; join with sl st to first sc. (8 sc) Fasten off Color A and weave in all ends.

ROUND 2: With right side facing, join Color B with sl st to any sc, ch 3 (counts as first dc, now and throughout), [yo, insert hook in same st as joining, pull up lp, yo, draw through 2 lps on hook] 2 times (3 lps on hook), yo and draw through all 3 lps (first 3-bob made), ch 2, [3-bob in next sc, ch 2] around; join with sl st to first dc (3rd ch of beg ch-3). (8 bobbles & 8 ch-2 sps) Fasten off Color B and weave in all ends.

ROUND 3: With right side facing, join Color C with sl st to any ch-2 sp, ch 5, 3dtr-bob in same sp, ch 5, sl st in same sp, [(sl st, ch 5, 3dtr-bob, ch 5, sl st) in next ch-2 sp] around, join with sl st at base of beg ch-5. (8 petals) Fasten off Color C and weave in all ends.

ROUND 4: With right side facing, using Color D, join with sc to top of any petal (bobble), ch 7, sc at base between petals (in bobble on Round 2), ch 7, sc in top of next petal, ch 5, *sc in top of next petal, ch 7, sc at base between petals, ch 7, sc in top of next petal, ch 5; rep from * around; join with sl st to first sc. (8 sc, 8 ch-7 lps & 4 ch-5 lps) Fasten off Color D and weave in all ends.

ROUND 5: With right side facing, join Color E with sl st to 2nd ch-7 lp, ch 3, 3 dc in same lp, ch 5, sc in next ch-5 lp, ch 5, 4 dc in next ch-7 lp, ch 5, *4 dc in next ch-7 lp, ch 5, sc in next ch-5 lp, ch 5, 4 dc in next ch-7 lp, ch 5; rep from * around; join with sl st to first dc (3rd ch of beg ch-3). (8 groups of 4-dc & 12 ch-5 lps) Fasten off Color E and weave in all ends.

ROUND 6: With right side facing, join Color A with sl st to 2nd ch-5 lp of any corner, ch 3, 3 dc in same lp, [ch 4, 4 dc in next ch-5 lp] 2 times, ch 3, *[4 dc in next ch-5 lp, ch 4] 2 times, 4 dc in next ch-5 lp, ch 3; rep from * around; join with sl st to first dc (3rd ch of beg ch-3). (12 groups of 4-dc, 8 ch-4 lps & 4 ch-3 lps) Fasten off Color A and weave in all ends.

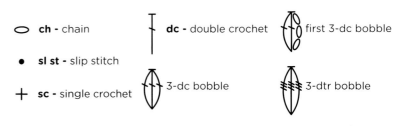

PATTERN

Base Round: Using Color A, ch 4; join with sl st to first ch to form a ring.

ROUND 1: (Right Side) Ch 3 (counts as first dc, now and throughout), 17 dc in ring; join with sl st to first dc (3rd ch of beg ch-3). (18 dc)

ROUND 2: Ch 1 (NOT counted as first st, now and throughout), sc in same st as joining, ch 5, [skip next 2 dc, sc in next dc, ch 5] around; join with sl st to first sc. (6 sc & 6 ch-5 lps) Fasten off Color A and weave in all ends.

ROUND 3: With right side facing, join Color B with sl st to first ch-5 lp, ch 1, (sc, hdc, dc, tr, dc, hdc, sc) in same lp, [(sc, hdc, dc, tr, dc, hdc, sc) in next ch-5 lp] around; join with sl st to first sc. (6 petals) Fasten off Color B and weave in all ends.

ROUND 4: With right side facing, join Color C with sl st to last sc of any petal, ch 3, [yo, insert hook in same sc, pull up lp, yo, draw through 2 lps on hook] 2 times (3 lps on hook), yo and draw through all 3 lps (first 3-bob made), ch 3, 3-bob in next sc (first sc of next petal), ch 2, skip next 2 sts, sc in next tr, ch 2, skip next 2 sts, *3-bob in next sc, ch 3, 3-bob in next sc, ch 2, skip next 2 sts, sc in next tr, ch 2, skip next 2 sts; rep from * around; join with sl st to first dc (3rd ch of beg ch-3). (12 bobbles, 6 sc, 12 ch-2 sps & 6 ch-3 sps) Fasten off Color C and weave in all ends.

ROUND 5: With right side facing, join Color D with sl st to any ch-3 sp (between bobbles), ch 3, [yo, insert hook in same sc, pull up lp, yo, draw through 2 lps on hook] 2 times (3 lps on hook), yo and draw through all 3 lps (first 3-bob made), ch 3, 3-bob in same sp, [ch 2, dc in next ch-2 sp] 2 times, ch 2, *(3-bob, ch 3, 3-bob) in next ch-3 sp, [ch 2, dc in next ch-2 sp] 2 times, ch 2; rep from * around; join with sl st to first dc (3rd ch of beg ch-3). (12 bobbles, 12 dc, 18 ch-2 sps & 6 ch-3 sps) Fasten off Color D and weave in all ends.

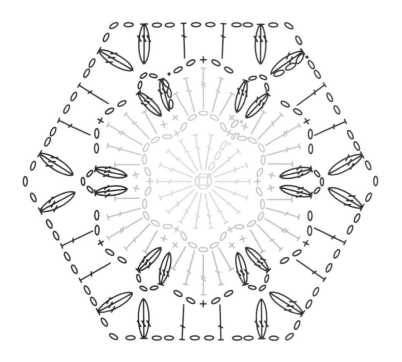

○ **ch -** chain

● **sl st -** slip stitch

✛ **sc -** single crochet

hdc - half double crochet

dc - double crochet

tr - treble crochet

 3-dc bobble

 first 3-dc bobble

PATTERN

Base Round: Using either Color A or Color B, ch 6; join with sl st to first ch to form a ring.

ROUND 1: (Right Side) Ch 3 (counts as first dc, now and throughout), yo, insert hook in ring, pull up lp, yo, draw through 2 lps on hook (2 lps on hook), yo and draw through all lps (first 2-bob made), ch 1, dc in ring, ch 1, [2-bob in ring, ch 1, dc in ring, ch 1] 7 times; join with sl st to first dc (3rd ch of beg ch-3). (8 bobbles, 8 dc & 16 ch-1 sps) Fasten off and weave in all ends.

ROUND 2: With right side facing, using next Color, join with sc to any ch-1 sp, ch 5, [sc in next ch-1 sp, ch 5] around; join with sl st to first sc. (16 sc & 16 ch-5 lps)

ROUND 3: Sl st in next ch-5 lp, ch 3 (counts as first dc, now and throughout), [yo, insert hook in same lp, pull up lp, yo, draw through 2 lps on hook] 2 times (3 lps on hook), yo and draw through all 3 lps (first 3-bob made), ch 5, 3-bob in same lp, ch 5, [in next lp, skip next 2 ch, sl st in next (center) ch, ch 5] 3 times, *(3-bob, ch 5, 3-bob) in next lp, ch 5, [sl st in center ch of next lp, ch 5] 3 times; rep from * around; join with sl st to first dc (3rd ch of beg ch-3). (8 bobbles & 20 ch-5 lps)

ROUND 4: Sl st in next ch-5 lp, ch 3, [yo, insert hook in same lp, pull up lp, yo, draw through 2 lps on hook] 2 times (3 lps on hook), yo and draw through all 3 lps (first 3-bob made), ch 5, 3-bob in same lp, ch 5, [sl st in center ch of next lp, ch 5] 4 times, *(3-bob, ch 5, 3-bob) in next lp, ch 5, [sl st in center ch of next lp, ch 5] 4 times; rep from * around; join with sl st to first dc (3rd ch of beg ch-3). (8 bobbles & 24 ch-5 lps) Fasten off and weave in all ends.

ch - chain

sl st - slip stitch

sc - single crochet

dc - double crochet

2-dc bobble

first 2-dc bobble

3-dc bobble

first 3-dc bobble

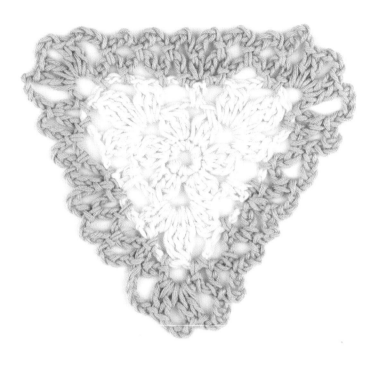

PATTERN

Base Round: Using Color A, ch 4; join with sl st to first ch to form a ring.

ROUND 1: (Right Side) Ch 1 (NOT counted as first st), 6 sc in ring; join with sl st to first sc. (6 sc)

ROUND 2: Ch 3 (counts as first dc, now and throughout), [yo, insert hook in same st as joining, pull up lp, yo, draw through 2 lps on hook] 2 times (3 lps on hook), yo and draw through all 3 lps (first 3-bob made), ch 3, [3-bob in next sc, ch 3] around; join with sl st to first dc (3rd ch of beg ch-3). (6 bobbles & 6 ch-3 sps)

ROUND 3: Sl st in next ch-3 sp, ch 3, [yo, insert hook in same st as joining, pull up lp, yo, draw through 2 lps on hook] 2 times (3 lps on hook), yo and draw through all 3 lps (first 3-bob made), ch 4, (3tr-bob, ch 4, 3-bob) in same sp, ch 3, sc in next ch-3 sp, ch 3, *(3-bob, ch 4, 3tr bob, ch 4, 3-bob) in next ch-3 sp, ch 3, sc in next ch-3 sp, ch 3; rep from * around; join with sl st to first dc (3rd ch of beg ch-3). (9 bobbles, 3 sc, 6 ch-4 sps & 6 ch-3 sps) Fasten off Color A and weave in all ends.

ROUND 4: With right side facing, join Color B with sl st to last ch-3 sp made (before first 3-bob of bobble group), ch 5, sl st in same sp, ch 5, [(sl st, ch 5, sl st) in next ch-sp, ch 5] 3 times, (sl st, ch 5, sl st) in next ch-3 sp, *[(sl st, ch 5, sl st) in next ch-sp, ch 5] 5 times, (sl st, ch 5, sl st) in next ch-3 sp; rep from * around; join with sl st in first ch. (18 ch-5 lps)

ROUND 5: *[Ch 5, sl st in next ch-5 lp] 3 times, ch 5, (2 dc, ch 5, 2 dc) in next ch-5 lp, [ch 5, sl st in next ch-5 lp] 3 times, ch 5, sl st in sp between next 2 sl sts; rep from * around. Fasten off Color B and weave in all ends.

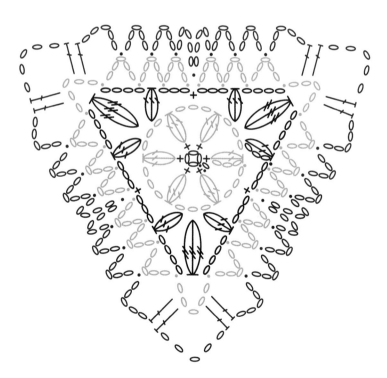

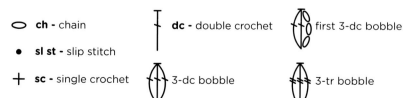

⬭ **ch** - chain   │ **dc** - double crochet   ◊ first 3-dc bobble

● **sl st** - slip stitch

✛ **sc** - single crochet   ◊ 3-dc bobble   ◊ 3-tr bobble

PATTERN

Base Round: Using Color A, ch 4; join with sl st to first ch to form a ring

ROUND 1: (Right Side) Ch 1 (NOT counted as first st), 8 sc in ring; join with sl st to first sc. (8 sc) Fasten off Color A and weave in all ends.

ROUND 2: With right side facing, join Color B with sl st to any sc, ch 4, 3tr-bob in same sc, ch 4, sl st in same sc, [(sl st, ch 4, 3tr-bob, ch 4, sl st) in next sc] around; join with sl st to first ch. (8 petals) Fasten off Color B and weave in all ends.

ROUND 3: With right side facing, join Color C with sl st to any sl st (between petals), ch 3 (counts as first dc, now and throughout), dc in same st, ch 3, *2 dc in next sl st (between petals), ch 3; rep from * around; join with sl st to first dc (3rd ch of beg ch-3). (16 dc & 8 ch-3 sps) Fasten off Color C and weave in all ends.

ROUND 4: With right side facing, join Color D with sl st to any ch-3 sp, ch 3, (2 dc, ch 1, 3 dc) in same sp, ch 2, sc in next ch-3 sp, ch 2, *(3 dc, ch 1, 3 dc) in next ch-3 sp, ch 2, sc in next ch-3 sp, ch 2; rep from * around; join with sl st to first dc (3rd ch of beg ch-3). (24 dc, 4 ch-1 sps, 4 sc & 8 ch-2 sps) Fasten off Color D and weave in all ends.

⬭ **ch -** chain   ✛ **sc -** single crochet   ⬙ **3-tr bobble**

• **sl st -** slip stitch   ┼ **dc -** double crochet

MOTIF 13

⬭ **ch** - chain

● **sl st** - slip stitch

✛ **sc** - single crochet

† **hdc** - half double crochet

† **dc** - double crochet

PATTERN

Base Round: Using Color A, ch 4; join with sl st to first ch to form a ring.

ROUND 1: (Right Side) Ch 1 (NOT counted as first st, now and throughout), 8 sc in ring; join with sl st to first sc. (8 sc)

ROUND 2: Ch 1, sc in same st as joining, ch 5, [sc in next sc, ch 5] around; join with sl st to first sc. (8 sc & 8 ch-5 lps)
Fasten off Color A and weave in all ends.

ROUND 3: With right side facing, join Color B with sl st to any ch-5 lp, ch 3 (counts as first dc), (dc, ch 1, 2 dc) in same lp, 2 hdc in next ch-5 lp, *(2 dc, ch 1, 2 dc) in next ch-5 lp, 2 hdc in next ch-5 lp; rep from * around; join with sl st to first dc (3rd ch of beg ch-3).
Fasten off Color B and weave in all ends.

PATTERN

Base Round: Using Color A, ch 4; join with sl st to first ch to form a ring.

ROUND 1: (Right Side) Ch 3 (counts as first dc, now and throughout), yo, insert hook in ring, pull up lp, yo, draw through 2 lps on hook (2 lps on hook), yo and draw through all lps (first 2-bob made), ch 3, [2-bob in ring, ch 3] 5 times; join with sl st to first dc (3rd ch of beg ch-3). (6 bobbles & 6 ch-3 sps)

ROUND 2: Ch 6, (counts as first dc & ch-3, now and throughout), dc in same st as joining, 2 dc in next ch-3 sp, *(dc, ch 3, dc) in next bobble, 2 dc in next ch-3 sp; rep from * around; join with sl st to first dc (3rd ch of beg ch-6). (24 dc & 6 ch-3 sps)

ROUND 3: Sl st in ch-3 sp, ch 6, dc in same sp, dc in each of next 4 dc, *(dc, ch 3, dc) in next ch-3 sp, dc in each of next 4 dc; rep from * around; join with sl st to first dc (3rd ch of beg ch-6). (36 dc & 6 ch-3 sps)

ROUND 4: Sl st in ch-3 sp, ch 6, dc in same sp, dc in each of next 6 dc, *(dc, ch 3, dc) in next ch-3 sp, dc in each of next 6 dc; rep from * around; join with sl st to first dc (3rd ch of beg ch-6). (48 dc & 6 ch-3 sps)

ROUND 5: Sl st in ch-3 sp, ch 6, dc in same sp, dc in each of next 8 dc, *(dc, ch 3, dc) in next ch-3 sp, dc in each of next 8 dc; rep from * around; join with sl st to first dc (3rd ch of beg ch 6). (60 dc & 6 ch-3 sps) Fasten off Color A and weave in all ends.

ROUND 6: With right side facing, join Color B with sl st to any ch-3 sp, ch 1 (NOT counted as first st), sc in same st, 3 sc in next sp, sc in each of next 10 sc, *3 sc in next corner ch-3 sp, sc in each of next 10 sc; rep from * around; join with sl st to first sc. (78 sc) Fasten off Color B and weave in all ends.

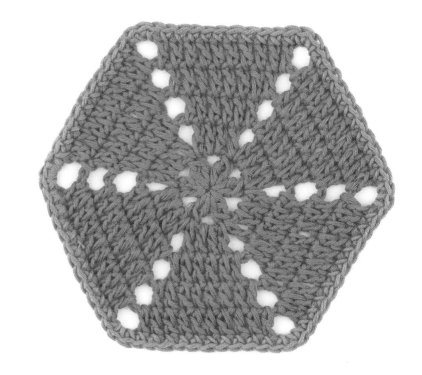

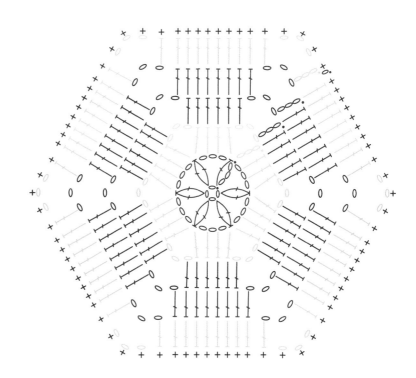

⬭ **ch -** chain	⊥ **dc -** double crochet	⬮ **first 2-dc bobble**
● **sl st -** slip stitch		
+ **sc -** single crochet	⬮ **2-dc bobble**	

59

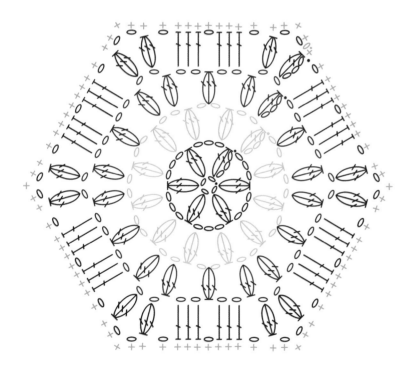

PATTERN

Base Round: Using Color A, ch 4; join with sl st to first ch to form a ring.

ROUND 1: (Right Side) Ch 3 (counts as first dc, now and throughout), [yo, insert hook in ring, pull up lp, yo, draw through 2 lps on hook] 2 times (3 lps on hook), yo and draw through all 3 lps (first 3-bob made), ch 3, [3 bob in ring, ch 3] 5 times; join with sl st to first dc (3rd ch of beg ch-3). (6 bobbles & 6 ch-3 sps) Fasten off Color A and weave in all ends.

ROUND 2: With right side facing, join Color B with sl st to any ch-3 sp, ch 3, [yo, insert hook in same sp, pull up lp, yo, draw through 2 lps on hook] 2 times (3 lps on hook), yo and draw through all 3 lps (first 3-bob made), ch 2, 3-bob in next sp, ch 2, 3-bob in same sp, ch 2, *(3-bob, ch 2, 3-bob) in next ch-3 sp, ch 2; rep from * around; (3-bob, ch 2) in next ch-3 sp, join with sl st to first dc (3rd ch of beg ch-3). (12 bobbles & 12 ch-2 sps)

ROUND 3: Sl st in next ch-2 sp, ch 3, [yo, insert hook in same sp, pull up lp, yo, draw through 2 lps on hook] 2 times (3 lps on hook), yo and draw through all 3 lps (first 3-Bobble made), ch 2, 3-bob in same sp, ch 2, 3-bob in next ch-2 sp, ch 2, *(3 bob, ch 2, 3-bob) in next ch-2 sp, ch 2, 3-bob in next ch-2 sp, ch 2; rep from * around; join with sl st to first dc (3rd ch of beg ch-3). (18 bobbles & 18 ch-2 sps)

ROUND 4: Sl st in next ch-2 sp, ch 3, [yo, insert hook in same sp, pull up lp, yo, draw through 2 lps on hook] 2 times, yo and draw through all 3 lps (first 3-bob made), ch 2, 3-bob in same sp, ch 1, [3 dc in next ch-2 sp, ch 1] 2 times, *(3-bob, ch 2, 3-bob) in next ch-2 sp, ch 1, [3 dc in next ch-2 sp, ch 1] 2 times; rep from * around; join with sl st to first dc (3rd ch of beg ch-3). (12 bobbles, 36 dc, 18 ch-1 sps & 6 ch-2 sps) Fasten off Color B and weave in all ends.

ROUND 5: With right side facing, join Color C with sl st to any corner ch-2 sp, ch 1 (NOT counted as first st), 3 sc in same sp, [sc in next st or sp] around, working 3 sc in each corner ch-2 sp; join with sl st to first sc. (84 sc) Fasten off Color C and weave in all ends.

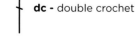 **ch -** chain	**dc -** double crochet	 first 3-dc bobble
● **sl st -** slip stitch		
+ **sc -** single crochet	3-dc bobble	

PATTERN

Base Round: Using Color A, ch 4; join with sl st to first ch to form a ring.

ROUND 1: (Right Side) Ch 3 (counts as first dc, now and throughout), [yo, insert hook in ring, pull up lp, yo, draw through 2 lps on hook] 2 times (3 lps on hook), yo and draw through all 3 lps (first 3-bob made), ch 3, [3 bob in ring, ch 3] 5 times; join with sl st to first dc (3rd ch of beg ch-3). (6 bobbles & 6 ch-3 sps)

ROUND 2: Ch 3, [yo, insert hook in same st as joining, pull up lp, yo, draw through 2 lps on hook] 2 times (3 lps on hook), yo and draw through all 3 lps (first 3-bob made), ch 2, 3-bob in next ch-3 sp, ch 2, *3-bob in next bobble, ch 2, 3-bob in next ch-3 sp, ch 2; rep from * around; join with sl st to first dc (3rd ch of beg ch-3). (12 bobbles & 12 ch-2 sps)

ROUND 3: Ch 3, [yo, insert hook in same st as joining, pull up lp, yo, draw through 2 lps on hook] 2 times (3 lps on hook), yo and draw through all 3 lps (first 3-bob made), ch 2, [dc in next ch-2 sp, ch 2] 2 times, *3-bob in next bobble, ch 2, [dc in next ch-2 sp, ch 2] 2 times; rep from * around; join with sl st to first dc (3rd ch of beg ch-3). (6 bobbles, 12 dc & 18 ch-2 sps)

ROUND 4: Ch 3, [yo, insert hook in same st as joining, pull up lp, yo, draw through 2 lps on hook] 2 times (3 lps on hook), yo and draw through all 3 lps (first 3-bob made), ch 2, dc in next ch-2 sp, ch 2, 3-bob in next ch-2 sp, ch 2, dc in next ch-2 sp, ch2, *3-bob in next bobble, ch 2, dc in next ch-2 sp, ch 2, 3-bob in next ch-2 sp, ch 2, dc in next ch-2 sp, ch2; rep from * around; join with sl st to first dc (3rd ch of beg ch-3). (12 bobbles, 12 dc & 24 ch-2 sps) Fasten off Color A and weave in all ends.

ROUND 5: With right side facing, using Color B, join with sc to any ch-2 sp, 2 sc in same sp, [3 sc in next ch-2 sp] around; join with sl st to first sc. (72 sc)

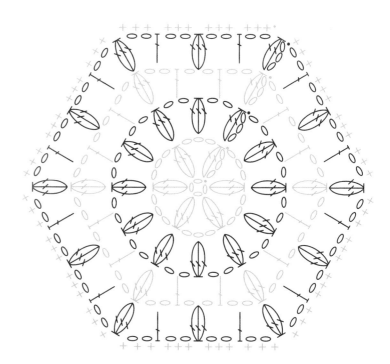

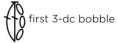

ch - chain

sl st - slip stitch

sc - single crochet

dc - double crochet

first 3-dc bobble

3-dc bobble

MOTIF 17

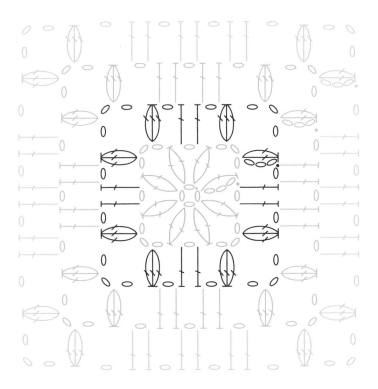

PATTERN

Base Round: Using Color A, ch 4; join with sl st to first ch to form a ring.

ROUND 1: (Right Side) Ch 3 (counts as first dc, now and throughout), yo, insert hook in ring, pull up lp, yo, draw through 2 lps on hook (2 lps on hook), yo and draw through both lps (first 2-bob made), ch 3, 2-bob in ring, ch 1 *2-bob in ring, ch 3, 2-bob in ring, ch 3; rep from * 2 times more; join with sl st to first dc (3rd ch of beg ch-3). (8 bobbles, 4 ch-3 sps & 4 ch-1 sps)

ROUND 2: Sl st in first ch-3 sp, ch 3, [yo, insert hook in same sp, pull up lp, yo, draw through 2 lps on hook] 2 times (3 lps on hook), yo and draw through all 3 lps (first 3-bob made), ch 3, 3-bob in same sp, ch 1, 2 dc in next ch-1 sp, ch 1, * (3-bob, ch 3, 3-bob) in next ch-3 sp, ch 1, 2 dc in next ch-1 sp, ch 1; rep from * around; join with sl st to first dc (3rd ch of beg ch-3). (8 bobbles, 8 dc, 8 ch-1 sps & 4 ch-3 sps)

ROUND 3: Sl st in first ch-3 sp, ch 3, [yo, insert hook in same sp, pull up lp, yo, draw through 2 lps on hook] 2 times (3 lps on hook), yo and draw through all 3 lps (first 3-bob made), ch 3, 3-bob in same sp, ch 1, [2 dc in next ch-1 sp, ch 1] 2 times, * (3-bob, ch 3, 3-bob) in next ch-3 sp, ch 1, [2 dc in next ch-1 sp,ch 1] 2 times; rep from * around; join with sl st to first dc (3rd ch of beg ch-3). (8 bobbles, 16 dc, 12 ch-1 sps & 4 ch-3 sps)

ROUND 4: Sl st in first ch-3 sp, ch 3, [yo, insert hook in same sp, pull up lp, yo, draw through 2 lps on hook] 2 times (3 lps on hook), yo and draw through all 3 lps (first 3-bob made), ch 3, 3-bob in same sp, ch 1, [2 dc in next ch-1 sp, ch 1] 3 times, * (3-bob, ch 3, 3-bob) in next ch-3 sp, ch 1, [2 dc in next ch-1 sp,ch 1] 3 times; rep from * around; join with sl st to first dc (3rd ch of beg ch-3). (8 bobbles, 24 dc, 16 ch-1 sps & 4 ch-3 sps) Fasten off and weave in all ends.

Popcorn (PC): 3 dc in same st or sp indicted, drop lp from hook, insert hook from front to back in first dc made, pull dropped lp through.

Note: The first Popcorn Stitch in a round is started differently to subsequent popcorns in round. Instructions for the first popcorn are included within the pattern. For subsequent popcorns follow the instructions above.

PATTERN

Base Round: Using Color A, ch 4; join with sl st to first ch to form a ring.

ROUND 1: (Right Side) Ch 3 (counts as first dc, now and throughout), 2 dc in ring, drop lp from hook, insert hook from front to back in first dc (3rd ch of beg ch-3), pull dropped lp through (first popcorn made), ch 1, dc in ring, ch 1, PC in ring, ch 3, * PC in ring, ch 1, dc in ring, ch 1, PC in ring, ch 3; rep from * around; join with sl st to first dc (3rd ch of beg ch-3). (8 popcorns, 4 dc, 8 ch-1 sps & 4 ch-3 sps)

ROUND 2: Sl st in next ch-1 sp, ch 6 (counts as first dc & ch-3), sc in next dc, ch 3, dc in next ch-1 sp, ch 2, (PC, ch 3, PC) in next ch-3 sp, ch 2, *dc in next ch-1 sp, ch 3, sc in next dc, ch 3, dc in next ch-1 sp, ch 2, (PC, ch 3, PC) in next ch-3 sp, ch 2; rep from * around; join with sl st to first dc (3rd ch of beg ch-3). (8 popcorns, 8 dc, 4 sc, 8 ch-2 sps & 12 ch-3 sps)

ROUND 3: Sl st in next ch-3 sp (before sc), ch 5 (counts as first dc & ch-2), dc in next ch-3 sp (after sc), ch 2, dc in next ch-2 sp, ch 2, (PC, ch 3, PC) in next ch-3 sp, ch 2, dc om next ch-2 sp, ch 2, *[dc in next ch-3 sp, ch2] 2 times, dc in next ch-2 sp, ch 2, (PC, ch 3, PC) in next ch-3 sp, ch 2; rep from * around; join with sl st to first dc (3rd ch of beg ch-3). (8 popcorns, 16 dc, 20 ch-2 sps & 4 ch-3 sps) Fasten off and weave in all ends.

ch - chain

sl st - slip stitch

sc - single crochet

dc - double crochet

first popcorn stitch

pc - popcorn stitch

MOTIF 19

PATTERN

Base Round: Using Color A, ch 4; join with sl st to first ch to form a ring.

ROUND 1: (Right Side) Ch 1 (NOT counted as first st), 8 sc in ring; join with sl st to first sc. (8 sc)

ROUND 2: *Ch 9, sl st in each of next 2 sc; rep from * around (the last sl st will be at base of beg ch-9). (4 ch-9 lps)

ROUND 3: Sl st in ch-9 lp, ch 3 (counts as first dc, now and throughout), (15 dc, sl st) in same lp, *(sl st, ch 3, 15 dc, sl st) in next ch-9 lp; rep from * around; join with sl st to first sl st. (4 petals – with 16 dc each)

ROUND 4: Ch 6 (counts as first dc & ch-3), skip first 3 dc, sc in next (4th) dc, ch 3, skip next 3 dc, (dc, ch 3, dc) in next (8th) dc, ch 3, skip next 3 dc, sc in next (12th) dc, ch 3, *dc between petals, ch 3, skip next 3 dc, sc in next dc, ch 3, skip next 3 dc, (dc, ch 3, dc) in next dc, ch 3, skip next 3 dc, sc in next dc, ch 3; rep from * around; join with sl st to first dc (3rd ch of beg ch-3). Fasten off and weave in all ends.

○ **ch -** chain   **+** **sc -** single crochet

● **sl st -** slip stitch   **dc -** double crochet

PATTERN

Base Round: Using Color A, ch 4; join with sl st to first ch to form a ring.

ROUND 1: (Right Side) Ch 1 (NOT counted as first st, now and throughout), 8 sc in ring; join with sl st to first sc. (8 sc) Fasten off Color A and weave in all ends.

ROUND 2: With right side facing, join Color B with sl st to any sc, [ch 5, sl st in each of next 2 sc] around (the last sl st will be at base of beg ch-5). (4 ch-5 lps)

ROUND 3: *(Sl st, ch 1, 7 dc, sl st) in next ch-5 lp, sc between lps; rep from * around; join with sl st to first sl st. (4 petals) Fasten off Color B and weave in all ends.

ROUND 4: With right side facing, join Color A with sl st to any sc, ch 6 (counts as first dc and ch 3), skip next 2 dc, sc in next (3rd) dc, ch 2, sc in next dc, ch 3, *skip next 3 dc, dc in next sc, ch 3, skip next 2 dc, sc in next dc, ch 2, sc in next dc, ch 3; rep from * around; join with sl st to first dc (3rd ch of beg ch-3). (4 dc, 8 sc, 4 ch-2 sps & 8 ch-3 sps)

ROUND 5: Ch 1, *3 sc in next ch-3 sp, (sc, ch 1, sc) in next ch-2 sp, 3 sc in next ch-3 sp; rep from * around; join with sl st to first sc. (32 sc & 4 ch-1 sps) Fasten off Color A and weave in all ends.

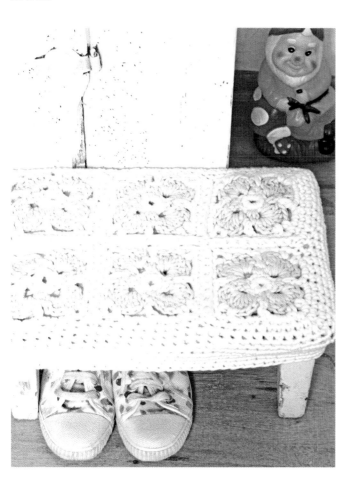

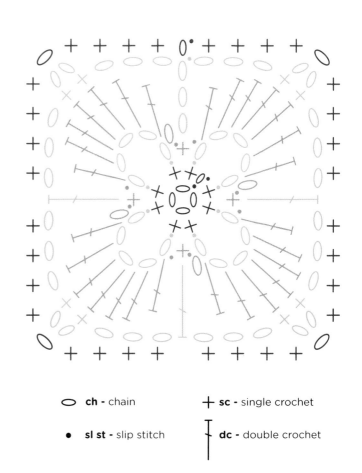

○ **ch -** chain   + **sc -** single crochet

● **sl st -** slip stitch   † **dc -** double crochet

MOTIF 21

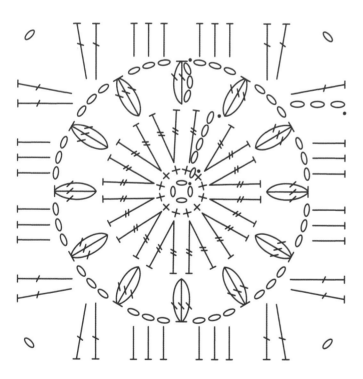

PATTERN

Base Round: Using Color A, ch 4; join with sl st to first ch to form a ring.

ROUND 1: (Right Side) Ch 1 (NOT counted as first st), 12 sc in ring; join with sl st to first sc. (12 sc) Fasten off Color A and weave in all ends. Join with a sl st into top of beginning ch-1. Fasten off.

ROUND 2: With right side facing, join Color B with sl st to any sc, ch 4 (counts as first tr), tr in same st as joining, [2 tr in next sc] around; join with sl st to first tr (4th ch of beg ch-4). (24 tr) Fasten off Color B and weave in all ends.

ROUND 3: With right side facing, join Color C with sl st to sp between any 2-tr group, ch 3 (counts as first dc, now and throughout), [yo, insert hook in same st as joining, pull up lp, yo, draw through 2 lps on hook] 2 times (3 lps on hook), yo and draw through all 3 lps (first 3-bob made), ch 3, *3-bob in next sp between 2-tr groups, ch 3; rep from * around; join with sl st to first dc (3rd ch of beg ch-3). (12 bobbles & 12 ch-3 sps) Fasten off Color C and weave in all ends.

ROUND 4: With right side facing, join Color D with sl st in any ch-3 sp, ch 3, (dc, ch 1, 2 dc) in same sp, 3 hdc in each of next 2 ch-3 sps, *(2 dc, ch 1, 2 dc) in next ch-3 sp, 3 hdc in each of next 2 ch-3 sps; rep from * around; join with sl st to first dc (3rd ch of beg ch-3). (16 dc, 24 hdc & 4 ch-1 sps) Fasten off Color D and weave in all ends.

⬭ **ch -** chain

● **sl st -** slip stitch

+ **sc -** single crochet

| **hdc -** half double crochet

† **dc -** double crochet

‡ **tr -** treble crochet

 **3-dc bobble**

 **first 3-dc bobble**

PATTERN

Base Round: Using Color A, ch 4; join with sl st to first ch to form a ring.

ROUND 1: (Right Side) Ch 1 (NOT counted as first st), 8 sc in ring; join with sl st to first sc. (8 sc)

ROUND 2: Ch 9 (counts as first tr & ch-5), 3tr-bob in next sc, ch 5, *tr in next sc, ch 5, 3tr-bob in next sc, ch 5; rep from * around; join with sl st to first tr (4th ch of beg ch-9). (4 bobbles, 4 tr & 8 ch-5 lps).

ROUND 3: Ch 7 (counts as first tr & ch-4), tr in same st as joining, ch 5, sc in next ch-5 lp, ch 5, sc in next bobble, ch 5, sc in next ch-5 lp, ch 5, *(tr, ch 3, tr) in next tr, ch 5, sc in next ch-5 lp, ch 5, sc in next bobble, ch 5, sc in next ch-5 lp, ch 5; rep from * around; join with sl st to first tr (4th ch of beg ch-4). (8 tr, 12 sc, 16 ch-5 lps & 4 ch-3 sps) Fasten off and weave in all ends.

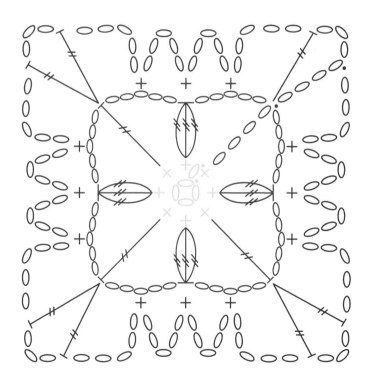

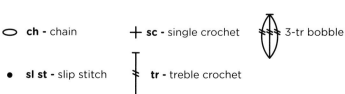

ch - chain   sc - single crochet   3-tr bobble

sl st - slip stitch   tr - treble crochet

MOTIF 23

3-Treble Cluster (3tr-cl): Wrap yarn twice around hook, insert hook into st or sp indicated, pull up lp (4 lps on hook), [yo, draw through 2 lps on hook] 2 times (2 lps on hook), *wrap yarn twice around hook, insert hook in next st or sp, pull up lp, [yo, draw through 2 lps on hook] 2 times, rep from * once more (4 lps on hook), yo and draw through all 4 lps.

Note: The first Cluster Stitch in a round is started differently to subsequent stitches in round. Instructions for the cluster are included within the pattern. For subsequent stitches follow the instructions above.

PATTERN

Base Round: Using Color A, ch 6; join with sl st to first ch to form a ring.

ROUND 1: (Right Side) Ch 1 (NOT counted as first st), 18 sc in ring; join with sl st to first sc. (18 sc)

ROUND 2: Ch 4 (counts as first tr), *wrap yarn twice around hook, insert hook in next st, pull up lp, [yo, draw through 2 lps on hook] 2 times, rep from * once more (3 lps on hook), yo and draw through all 3 lps (first cluster made), ch 5, *3tr-cl (using next 3 sc), ch 5; rep from * around; join with sl st to first tr (4th ch of beg ch-4). (6 clusters & 6 ch-5 lps)

ROUND 3: Ch 3 (counts as first dc), [yo, insert hook in same st as joining, pull up lp, yo, draw through 2 lps on hook] 2 times (3 lps on hook), yo and draw through all 3 lps (first 3-bob made), ch 3, 3-bob in same st, ch 1, 3 dc in next ch-5 lp, ch 1, *(3-bob, ch 3, 3-bob) in next cluster, ch 1, 3 dc in next ch-5 lp, ch 1; rep from * around; join with sl st to first dc (3rd ch of beg ch). (12 bobbles, 18 dc, 12 ch-1 sps & 6 ch-3 sps) Fasten off and weave in all ends.

 ch - chain

sl st - slip stitch

 sc - single crochet

 **dc -** double crochet

 first 3-dc bobble

first 3-tr cluster

 3-dc bobble

3-tr cluster

MOTIF 24

PATTERN

Base Round: Using Color A, ch 4; join with sl st to first ch to form a ring

ROUND 1: (Right Side) Ch 1 (NOT counted as first st), 12 sc in ring; join with sl st to first sc. (12 sc)

ROUND 2: Ch 4 (counts as first tr), *wrap yarn twice around hook, insert hook in same st as joining, pull up lp, [yo, draw through 2 lps on hook] 2 times, rep from * once more (3 lps on hook), yo and draw through all 3 lps (first bobble made), ch 5, [3tr bob in next sc, ch 5] around; join with sl st to first tr (4th ch of beg ch-4). (12 bobbles & 12 ch-5 lps) Fasten off Color A and weave in all ends.

ROUND 3: With right side facing, join Color B with sl st to any ch-5 lp, ch 6 (counts as first dc & ch-3), dc in same lp, ch 5, [sc in next lp, ch 5] 2 times, *(dc, ch 3, dc) in next ch-5 lp, ch 5, [sc in next lp, ch 5] 2 times; rep from * around; join with sl st to first dc (3rd ch of beg ch-6). (8 dc, 4 ch-3 sps, 8 sc & 12 ch-5 lps) Fasten off and weave in all ends.

 ch - chain

● **sl st -** slip stitch

✛ **sc -** single crochet

| **dc -** double crochet

 first 3-tr bobble

 3-tr bobble

MOTIF 25

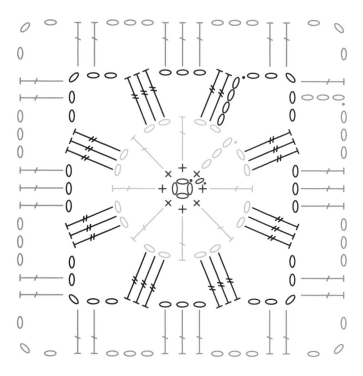

PATTERN

Base Round: Using Color A, ch 4; join with sl st to first ch to form a ring.

ROUND 1: (Right Side) Ch 1 (NOT counted as first st), 8 sc in ring; join with sl st to first sc. (8 sc) Fasten off Color A and weave in all ends.

ROUND 2: With right side facing, join Color B with sl st to any sc, ch 5 (counts as first dc & ch-2), [dc in next sc, ch 2] around; join with sl st to first dc (3rd ch of beg ch-5). (8 dc & 8 ch-2 sps) Fasten off Color B and weave in all ends.

ROUND 3: With right side facing, join Color C with sl st to any ch-2 sp, ch 4 (counts as first tr), 2 tr in same sp, ch 3, 3 tr in next ch-2 sp, ch 5, *3 tr in next ch-2 sp, ch 3, 3 tr in next ch-2 sp, ch 5; rep from * around; join with sl st to first tr (4th ch of beg ch-4). (24 tr, 4 ch-3 sps & 4 ch-5 lps) Fasten off Color C and weave in all ends.

ROUND 4: With right side facing, join Color D with sl st to any ch-5 lp, ch 3 (counts as first dc), (dc, ch 3, 2 dc) in same lp, ch 3, 3 dc in next ch-3 sp, ch 3, *(2 dc, ch 3, 2 dc) in next ch-5 lp, ch 3, 3 dc in next ch-3 sp, ch 3; rep from * around; join with sl st to first dc (3rd ch of beg ch-3). (28 dc & 12 ch-3 sps) Fasten off Color D and weave in all ends.

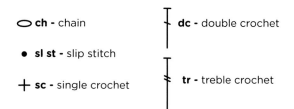

⬭ **ch -** chain

● **sl st -** slip stitch

✚ **sc -** single crochet

dc - double crochet

tr - treble crochet

70

MOTIF 26

3-Treble Cluster (3tr-cl): Wrap yarn twice around hook, insert hook into st or sp indicated, pull up lp (4 lps on hook), [yo, draw through 2 lps on hook] 2 times (2 lps on hook), *wrap yarn twice around hook, insert hook in next st or sp, pull up lp, [yo, draw through 2 lps on hook] 2 times, rep from * once more (4 lps on hook), yo and draw through all 4 lps.

Note: The first Cluster Stitch in a round is started differently to subsequent clusters in round. Instructions for the first cluster are included within the pattern. For subsequent clusters follow the instructions above.

PATTERN

Base Round: Using Color A, ch 6; join with sl st to first ch to form a ring.

ROUND 1: (Right Side) Ch 1 (NOT counted as first st, now and throughout), 18 sc in ring; join with sl st to first sc. (18 sc) Fasten off Color A and weave in all ends.

ROUND 2: With right side facing, join Color B with sl st to any sc, ch 4 (counts as first tr), *wrap yarn twice around hook, insert hook in next st, pull up lp, [yo, draw through 2 lps on hook] 2 times, rep from * once more (3 lps on hook), yo and draw through all 3 lps (first cluster made), ch 5, *3tr-cl (using next 3 sc), ch 5; rep from * around; join with sl st to first tr (4th ch of beg ch-4). (6 clusters & 6 ch-5 lps) Fasten off Color B and weave in all ends.

ROUND 3: With right side facing, join Color C with sl st to any ch-5 lp, ch 1, sc in same lp, ch 7, (dc, ch 3, dc in next lp, ch 7, *sc in next lp, ch 7, (dc, ch 3, dc) in next lp, ch 7; rep from * around; join with sl st to first sc. (3 sc, 6 ch-7 lps, 6 dc & 3 ch-3 sps) Fasten off Color C and weave in all ends.

ROUND 4: With right side facing, join Color D with sl st to any ch-3 sp, ch 3 (counts as first dc), [yo, insert hook in ring, pull up lp, yo, draw through 2 lps on hook] 2 times (3 lps on hook), yo and draw through all 3 lps (first 3-bob made), ch 4, (3tr bob, ch 4, 3-bob) in same sp, ch 5, sc in next ch-7 lp, ch 5, (dc, ch 3, dc) in next sc, ch 5, sc in next ch-7 lp, ch 5, *(3-bob, ch 4, 3tr-bob, ch 4, 3-bob) in next ch-3 sp, ch 5, sc in next ch-7 lp 5, (dc, ch 3, dc) in next sc, ch 5, sc in next ch-7 lp, ch 5; rep from * around; join with sl st to first dc. (9 bobbles, 6 dc, 6 sc, 3 ch-3 sps, 6 ch-4 lps & 12 ch-5 lps) Fasten off Color D and weave in all ends.

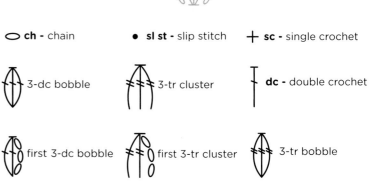

⬭ **ch** - chain	● **sl st** - slip stitch	✚ **sc** - single crochet
3-dc bobble	3-tr cluster	**dc** - double crochet
first 3-dc bobble	first 3-tr cluster	3-tr bobble

MOTIF 27

Puff Stitch (puff): In same st or sp indicated, [yo hook, insert hook, pull up a loop (to height of dc)] 4 times, yo and draw through all 9 loops on the hook, ch 1 to secure.

PATTERN

Base Round: Using Color A, ch 4; join with sl st to first ch to form a ring.

ROUND 1: (Right Side) Ch 1 (NOT counted as first st), 12 sc in ring; join with sl st to first sc. (12 sc)

ROUND 2: Ch 2 (counts as first hdc, now and throughout), puff in same st as joining, [ch 2, puff in next sc] 2 times, ch 5, *puff in next sc, [ch 2, puff in next sc] 2 times, ch 5; rep from * around; join with sl st to first puff. (12 puffs, 8 ch-2 sps & 4 ch-5 lps)

ROUND 3: Sl st in first ch-2 sp, ch 2, puff in same sp, ch 2, puff in next ch-2 sp, ch 1, (2 dc, ch 3, 2 dc) in next ch-5 lp, ch 1, *puff in next ch-2 sp, ch 2, puff in next ch-2 sp, ch 1, (2 dc, ch 3, 2 dc) in next ch-5 lp, ch 1; rep from * around; join with sl st to first puff. (8 puffs, 16 dc, 4 ch-2 sps, 8 ch-1 sps & 4 ch-3 sps)

ROUND 4: Sl st in next ch-2 sp, ch 2, puff in same sp, ch 1, dc in next ch-1 sp, dc in sp between next 2 dc, (2 dc, ch 3, 2 dc) in next ch-3 sp, dc in sp between next 2 dc, dc in next ch-1 sp, ch 1, *puff in next ch-2 sp, ch 1, dc in next ch-1 sp, dc in sp between next 2 dc, (2 dc, ch 3, 2 dc) in next ch-3 sp, dc in sp between next 2 dc, dc in next ch-1 sp, ch 1,; rep from * around; join with sl st to first puff. (4 puffs, 32 dc, 8 ch-1 sps & 4 ch-3 sps) Fasten off and weave in all ends.

○ **ch -** chain

● **sl st -** slip stitch

+ **sc -** single crochet

dc - double crochet

 puff stitch

 first puff stitch

MOTIF 28

PATTERN

Base Round: Using Color A, ch 4; join with sl st to first ch to form a ring.

ROUND 1: (Right Side) Ch 4 (counts as first tr), wrap yarn twice around hook, insert hook in ring, pull up lp, [yo, draw through 2 lps on hook] 2 times (2 lps on hook), yo and draw through both lps (first 2tr-bob made) ch 2, [2tr-bob in ring, ch 2] 7 times; join with sl st to first tr (4th ch of beg ch-4). (8 bobbles & 8 ch-2 sps) Fasten off Color A and weave in all ends.

ROUND 2: With right side facing, join Color B with sl st to any ch-2 sp, ch 3, (2tr-bob, ch 5, 2tr-bob, ch 3, sl st) in same sp, *(sl st, ch 3, 2tr-bob, ch 5, 2tr-bob, ch 3, sl st) in next ch-2 sp; rep from * around; join with sl st to first sl st. (16 bobbles, 16 ch-3 sps & 8 ch-5 lps) Fasten off Color B and weave in all ends.

ROUND 3: With RS facing, join color C to any ch-5 sp, ch 1, sc in same sp, *ch 8, sc 1 into next ch-5 sp, rep from * to end; join with sl st to first sc.

ROUND 4: Sl st to next ch-8 sp, ch 1 (not counted as first st), sc in same sp, hdc, dc 2, ch 2, dc 2, hdc, sc. *sc in next sp, hdc, dc 2, ch 2, dc 2, hdc, sc, rep from * to end; join with sl st to first sc. (8 petals) Fasten off color C and weave in all ends.

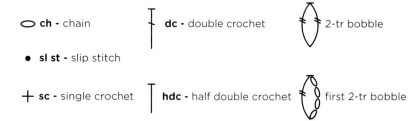

○ **ch -** chain | **dc -** double crochet   ◇ 2-tr bobble

● **sl st -** slip stitch

+ **sc -** single crochet | **hdc -** half double crochet   ◇ first 2-tr bobble

3-Treble Cluster (3tr-cl): Wrap yarn twice around hook, insert hook into st or sp indicated, pull up lp (4 lps on hook), [yo, draw through 2 lps on hook] 2 times (2 lps on hook), *wrap yarn twice around hook, insert hook in next st or sp, pull up lp, [yo, draw through 2 lps on hook] 2 times, rep from * once more (4 lps on hook), yo and draw through all 4 lps.

Note: The first Cluster Stitch in a round is started differently to subsequent clusters in round. Instructions for the first cluster are included within the pattern. For subsequent clusters follow the instructions above.

PATTERN

Base Round: Using Color A, ch 6; join with sl st to first ch to form a ring.

ROUND 1: (Right Side) Ch 3 (counts as first dc, now and throughout), 23 dc in ring; join with sl st to first dc (3rd ch of beg ch-3). (24 dc) Fasten off Color A and weave in all ends.

ROUND 2: With right side facing, join Color B with sl st to any dc, ch 6 (counts as first dc & ch 3), skip next dc, [dc in next dc, ch 3, skip next dc] around; join with sl st to first dc (3rd ch of beg ch-3). (12 dc & 12 ch-3 sps) Fasten off Color B and weave in all ends.

ROUND 3: With right side facing, join Color C with sl st to same st as joining, ch 1 (NOT counted as first st), [3 sc in next ch-3 sp] around; join with sl st to first sc. (36 sc)
Fasten off Color C and weave in all ends.

ROUND 4: With right side facing, join Color D with sl st to any sc, ch 4 (counts as first tr), *wrap yarn twice around hook, insert hook in next st, pull up lp, [yo, draw through 2 lps on hook] 2 times, rep from * once more (3 lps on hook), yo and draw through all 3 lps (first cluster made), ch 5, *3tr-cl (using next 3 sc), ch 5; rep from * around; join with sl st to first tr (4th ch of beg ch-4). (12 clusters & 12 ch-5 lps)

ROUND 5: Sl st in next ch-5 lp, (3 sc, ch 3, 3 sc) in same lp, *(3 sc, ch 3, 3 sc) in next ch-5 lp; rep from * around; join with sl st to first sc. (72 sc & 12 ch-3 sps) Fasten off Color D and weave in all ends.

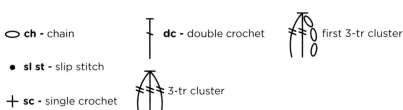

⬭ **ch -** chain

● **sl st -** slip stitch

✛ **sc -** single crochet

┃ **dc -** double crochet

⋔ **3-tr cluster**

⋔ **first 3-tr cluster**

MOTIF 30

PATTERN

Base Round: Using Color A, ch 4; join with sl st to first ch to form a ring.

ROUND 1: (Right Side) Ch 3 (counts as first dc, now and throughout), 3 dc in ring, ch 5, [4 dc in ring, ch 5] 3 times; join with sl st to first dc (3rd ch of beg ch-3). (16 dc & 4 ch-5 lps)

ROUND 2: Ch 8 (counts as first dc and ch-5, now and throughout), skip next 2 dc, sc in sp before next dc, skip next 2 dc, ch 5, *(2 dc, ch 3, 2 dc) in next ch-5 lp, ch 5, sc in center sp of next 4-dc group, ch 5; rep from * 2 times more, (2 dc, ch 3, dc) in last ch-5 lp; join with sl st to first dc (3rd ch of beg ch-8). (16 dc, 4 sc, 4 ch-3 sps &, 8 ch-5 lps)

ROUND 3: Ch 8, [sc in next ch-5 lp, ch 5] 2 times, *(2 dc, ch 3, 2 dc) in next ch-3 sp, ch 5, [sc in next ch-5 lp, ch 5] 2 times; rep from * 2 times more, (2 dc, ch 3, dc) in last ch-3 sp; join with sl st to first dc (3rd ch of beg ch-8). (16 dc, 8 sc, 12 ch-5 lps & 4 ch-3 sps) Fasten off and weave in all ends.

◯ **ch -** chain   ✛ **sc -** single crochet

● **sl st -** slip stitch   ∤ **dc -** double crochet

MOTIF 31

PATTERN

Base Round: Using Color A, ch 4; join with sl st to first ch to form a ring.

ROUND 1: (Right Side) Ch 1 (NOT counted as first st), 8 sc in ring; join with sl st to first sc. (8 sc)

ROUND 2: Ch 4 (counts as first tr), *wrap yarn twice around hook, insert hook in same st as joining, pull up lp, [yo, draw through 2 lps on hook] 2 times, rep from * once more (4 lps on hook), yo and draw through all 4 lps (first bobble made), ch 5, *4tr-bob in next sc, ch 5; rep from * around; join with sl st to first tr (4th ch of beg ch-4). (8 bobbles & 8 ch-5 lps) Fasten off and weave in all ends.

○ **ch -** chain

● **sl st -** slip stitch

+ **sc -** single crochet

✦ 4-tr bobble

✦ first 4-tr bobble

MOTIF 32

PATTERN

Base Round: Using Color A, ch 4; join with sl st to first ch to form a ring.

ROUND 1: (Right Side) Ch 4 (counts as first tr), 15 tr in ring; join with sl st to first tr (4th ch of beg ch-4). (16 tr) Fasten off Color A and weave in all ends.

ROUND 2: With right side facing, join Color B with sl st to any tr, ch 5 (counts as first dc & ch-2), [dc in next tr, ch 2] around; join with sl st to first dc (3rd ch of beg ch-5). (16 dc & 16 ch-2 sps) Fasten off Color B and weave in all ends.

ROUND 3: With right side facing, join Color C with sl st to any ch-2 sp, ch 3 (counts as first dc, now and throughout), [yo, insert hook in same sp, pull up lp, yo, draw through 2 lps on hook] 3 times (4 lps on hook), yo, draw through all 4 lps (first 4-bob made), ch 3; [4-bob in next ch-2 sp, ch 3] around; join with sl st to first dc (3rd ch of beg ch-3). (16 bobbles & 16 ch-3 sps) Fasten off Color C and weave in all ends.

ROUND 4: With right side facing, join Color D with sl st to any ch-3 sp, ch 3, 2 dc in same sp, 3 dc in next ch-3 sp, ch 3, *[3 dc in next ch-3 sp] 2 times, ch 3; rep from * around; join with sl st to first dc (3rd ch of beg ch-3). (48 dc & 8 ch-3 sps) Fasten off Color D and weave in all ends.

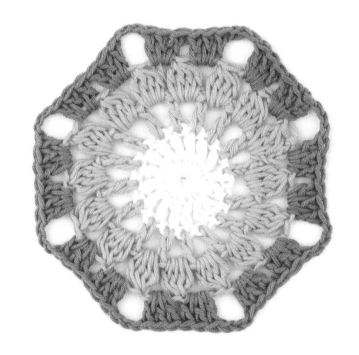

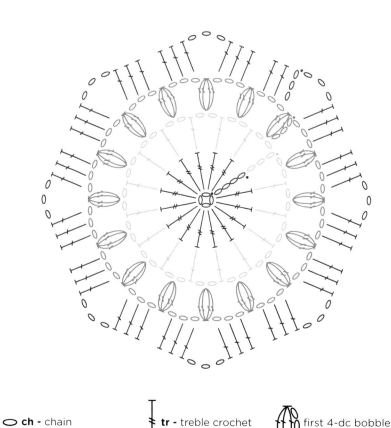

○ **ch -** chain

● **sl st -** slip stitch

dc - double crochet

tr - treble crochet

first 4-dc bobble

4-dc bobble

MOTIF 33

PATTERN

Base Round: Using Color A, ch 4; join with sl st to first ch to form a ring.

ROUND 1: (Right Side) Ch 8 (counts as first dc & ch-5), [dc in ring, ch 5] 7 times; join with sl st to first dc (3rd ch of beg ch-8). (8 dc & ch-5 lps) Fasten off Color A and weave in all ends.

ROUND 2: With right side facing, using Color B, join with sc to any ch-5 lp, (hdc, 2 dc, ch 1, 2 dc, hdc, sc) in same lp, *(sc, hdc, 2 dc, ch 1, 2 dc, hdc, sc) in next ch-5 lp; rep from * around; join with sl st to first sc. (8 petals) Fasten off Color B and weave in all ends.

ROUND 3: With right side facing, join Color C with sl st to any ch-1 sp, ch 1 (NOT counted as first st, now and throughout), sc in same sp, ch 6, [sc in next ch-1 sp, ch 6] around; join with sl st to first sc. (8 sc & 8 ch-6 lps)

ROUND 4: Sl st in next ch-6 lp, ch 1, 4 sc in same lp, ch 3, (3-bob, ch 5, 3-bob) in next ch-6 lp, ch 3, *4 sc in next lp, ch 3, (3-bob, ch 5, 3-bob) in next lp, ch 3; rep from * around; join with sl st to first sc. (8 bobbles, 16 sc, 8 ch-3 sps & 4 ch-5 lps) Fasten off Color C and weave in all ends.

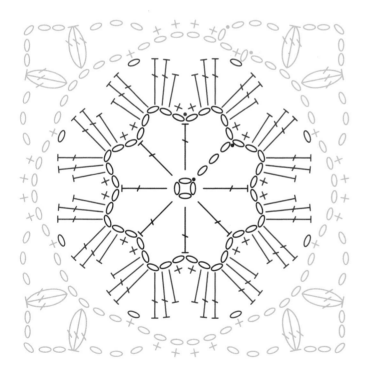

ch - chain

sl st - slip stitch

sc - single crochet

hdc - half double crochet

dc - double crochet

3-dc bobble

MOTIF 34

3-Double Crochet Cluster (3dc-cl): Yo, insert hook into st or sp indicated, pull up lp (3 lps on hook), yo, draw through 2 lps on hook (2 lps on hook), *yo, insert hook in next st or sp, pull up lp, yo, draw through 2 lps on hook; rep from * once more (4 lps on hook), yo and draw through all 4 lps.

Note: The first Cluster Stitch in a round is started differently to subsequent clusters in round. Instructions for the first cluster are included within the pattern. For subsequent clusters follow the instructions above.

PATTERN

Base Round: Using Color A, ch 5; join with sl st to first ch to form a ring.

ROUND 1: (Right Side) Ch 4 (counts as first tr), 23 tr in ring; join with sl st to first tr (4th ch of beg ch-4). (24 tr)

ROUND 2: Ch 3 (counts as first dc), dc in next 2 sts, ch 2, * dc in next 3 sts, ch 2. Repeat from * to end. Join with a sl st into top of first ch-3.

ROUND 3: Ch 3, dc in each of next 2 dc, ch 3, *dc in each of next 3 dc, ch 3; rep from * around; join with sl st to first dc. (24 dc & 8 ch-3 sps)

ROUND 4: Ch 3, [yo, insert hook in next dc, pull up lp, yo, draw through 2 lps on hook] 2 times (3 lps on hook), yo and draw through all 3 lps (first cluster made), ch 5, sc in next ch-3 sp, ch 5, *3dc-cl (using next 3 dc), ch 5, sc in next sp, ch 5; rep from * around; join with sl st to first dc. (8 clusters, 8 sc & 16 ch-5 lps) Fasten off and weave in all ends.

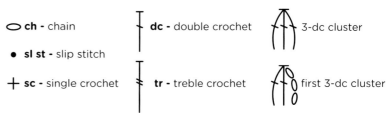

○ **ch -** chain

● **sl st -** slip stitch

✛ **sc -** single crochet

dc - double crochet

tr - treble crochet

3-dc cluster

first 3-dc cluster

MOTIF 35

PATTERN

Base Round: Using Color A, ch 4; join with sl st to first ch to form a ring.

ROUND 1: (Right Side) Ch 4 (counts as first tr, now and throughout), wrap yarn twice around hook, insert hook in ring, pull up lp, [yo, draw through 2 lps on hook] 2 times (2 lps on hook), yo and draw through both lps (first 2tr-bob made) ch 3, [2tr-bob in ring, ch 3] 5 times; join with sl st to first tr (4th ch of beg ch-4). (6 bobbles & 6 ch-3 sps)

ROUND 2: Sl st in next ch-3 sp, ch 1 (NOT counted as first st), 3 sc in same sp, ch 3, [3 sc in next sp, ch 3] around; join with sl st to first sc. (18 sc & 6 ch-3 sps)

ROUND 3: Sl st in each of next 3 sc, sl st in next ch-3 sp, ch 4, wrap yarn twice around hook, insert hook in same sp, pull up lp, [yo, draw through 2 lps on hook] 2 times (2 lps on hook), yo and draw through both lps (first 2tr-bob made), ch 3, 2tr-bob in same sp, ch 3, *(2tr-bob, ch 3, 2tr-bob) in next sp, ch 3; rep from * around; join with sl st to first tr (4th ch of beg ch-4). (12 bobbles & 12 ch-3 sps)

ROUND 4: Sl st in next ch-3 sp, ch 4, wrap yarn twice around hook, insert hook in same sp, pull up lp, [yo, draw through 2 lps on hook] 2 times (2 lps on hook), wrap yarn twice around hook, insert hook in same sp, pull up lp, [yo, draw through 2 lps on hook] 2 times (3 lps on hook), yo and draw through 3 lps (first 3tr-bob made), ch 3, 3tr-bob in same sp, ch 3, sc in next ch-3 sp, ch 3, *(3tr-bob, ch 3, 3tr-bob) in next sp, ch 3, sc in next sp, ch 3; rep from * around; join with sl st to first tr (4th ch of beg ch-4). (12 bobbles, 6 sc & 18 ch-3 sps) Fasten off and weave in all ends.

 ch - chain

sl st - slip stitch

sc - single crochet

 2-tr bobble   3-tr bobble

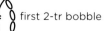 first 2-tr bobble

 first 3-tr bobble

MOTIF 36

PATTERN

Base Round: Using Color A, ch 4; join with sl st to first ch to form a ring.

ROUND 1: (Right Side) Ch 1 (NOT counted as first st, now and throughout), 12 sc in ring; join with sl st to first sc. (12 sc)

ROUND 2: Ch 3 (counts as first dc, now and throughout), yo, insert hook in same st as joining, pull up lp, yo, draw through 2 lps on hook (2 lps on hook), yo and draw through all lps (first 2-bob made), ch 2, [2-bob in next sc, ch 2] around; join with sl st to first dc (3rd ch of beg ch-3). (12 bobbles & 12 ch-2 sps)

ROUND 3: Sl st in next ch-2 sp, ch 1, sc in same sp, ch 5, [sc in next sp, ch 5] around; join with sl st to first sc. (12 sc & 12 ch-5 lps)

ROUND 4: Sl st in next ch-5 lp, ch 1, (sc, ch 7 sc) in same lp, ch 5, dc in next lp, ch 5, *(sc, ch 7, sc) in next lp, ch 5, dc in next lp, ch 5; rep from * around; join with sl st to first sc. (12 sc, 6 dc, 6 ch-7 lps & 12 ch-5 lps)

ROUND5: Sl st in next ch-7 lp, ch 3, (4 dc, ch 3, 5 dc) in same lp, 2 sc in next ch-5 lp, ch 1, 2 sc in next ch-5 lp, *(5 dc, ch 3, 5 dc) in next ch-7 lp, 2 sc in next lp, ch 1, 2 sc in next lp; rep from * around; join with sl st to first dc (3rd ch of beg ch-3). (60 dc, 6 ch-3 sps, 24 sc & 6 ch-1 sps)

ch - chain sc - single crochet 2-dc bobble

sl st - slip stitch dc - double crochet first 2-dc bobble

PATTERN

Base Round: Using Color A, ch 4; join with sl st to first ch to form a ring.

ROUND 1: (Right Side) Ch 1 (NOT counted as first st, now and throughout), 8 sc in ring; join with sl st to first sc. (8 sc)

ROUND 2: Ch 1, sc in same st as joining, ch 11, sc in next sc, *sc in next sc, ch 11, sc in next sc; rep from * around; join with sl st to first sc. (8 sc & 4 ch-11 lps)

ROUND 3: Sl st in next ch-11 sp, ch 1, (5 sc, ch 2, 5 sc) in same lp, *(5 sc, ch 2, 5 sc) in next lp; rep from * around; join with sl st to first sc. (40 sc & 4 ch-2 sps)

ROUND 4: Ch 6 (counts as first dc & ch-3), dc in same st as joining, ch 7, (3 dc, ch 3, 3 dc) in next ch-2 sp, ch 7, *(dc, ch 3, dc) in sp between petals, ch 7, (3 dc, ch 3, 3 dc) in next ch-2 sp, ch 7; rep from * around; join with sl st to first dc (3rd ch of beg ch-6). (32 dc, 8 ch-3 sps, & 8 ch-7 lps)

⬭ **ch -** chain

● **sl st -** slip stitch

✕ **sc -** single crochet

╪ **dc -** double crochet

PATTERN

Base Round: Using Color A, ch 4; join with sl st to first ch to form a ring

ROUND 1: (Right Side) Ch 3 (counts as first dc, now and throughout), [yo, insert hook in ring, pull up lp, yo, draw through 2 lps on hook] 2 times (3 lps on hook), yo and draw through all 3 lps (first 3-bob made), ch 3, [3 bob in ring, ch 3] 5 times; join with sl st to first dc (3rd ch of beg ch-3). (6 bobbles & 6 ch-3 sps)

ROUND 2: Sl st in next ch-3 sp, ch 3, [yo, insert hook in same sp, pull up lp, yo, draw through 2 lps on hook] 2 times (3 lps on hook), yo and draw through all 3 lps (first 3-bob made), ch 3, 3-bob in same sp, ch 3, 3-bob in next sp, ch 3, *(3-bob, ch 3, 3-bob) in next ch-3 sp, ch 3, 3-bob in next sp, ch 3; rep from * around; join with sl st to first dc (3rd ch of beg ch-3). (9 bobbles & 9 ch-3 sps)

ROUND 3: Sl st in next ch-3 sp, [yo, insert hook in same sp, pull up lp, yo, draw through 2 lps on hook] 2 times (3 lps on hook), yo and draw through all 3 lps (first 3-bob made), ch 3, 3-bob in same sp, ch 5, [sc in next sp, ch 5] 2 times, *(3-bob, ch 3, 3-bob) in next sp, ch 5, [sc in next sp, ch 5] 2 times; rep from * around; join with sl st to first dc (3rd ch of beg ch-3). (6 bobbles, 3 ch-3 sps, 6 sc & 9 ch-5 lps)

ROUND 4: Sl st in next ch-3 sp, [yo, insert hook in same sp, pull up lp, yo, draw through 2 lps on hook] 2 times (3 lps on hook), yo and draw through all 3 lps (first 3-bob made), ch 3, 3-bob in same sp, ch 5, [sc in next sp, ch 5] 3 times, *(3-bob, ch 3, 3-bob) in next sp, ch 5, [sc in next sp, ch 5] 3 times; rep from * around; join with sl st to first dc (3rd ch of beg ch-3). (6 bobbles, 3 ch-3 sps, 9 sc & 12 ch-5 lps) Fasten off and weave in all ends.

 ch - chain   3-dc bobble

• **sl st -** slip stitch

+ **sc -** single crochet   first 3-dc bobble

MOTIF 39

PATTERN

Base Round: Using Color A, ch 4; join with sl st to first ch to form a ring.

ROUND 1: (Right Side) Ch 4 (counts as first tr, now and throughout), wrap yarn twice around hook, insert hook in ring, pull up lp, [yo, draw through 2 lps on hook] 2 times (2 lps on hook), yo and draw through both lps (first 2tr-bob made) ch 3, 2tr-bob in ring, ch 5, *(2tr-bob, ch 3, 2tr-bob) in ring, ch 5; rep from * once more; join with sl st to first tr (4th ch of beg ch-4). (6 bobbles, 3 ch-3 sps & 3 ch-5 lps)

ROUND 2: Ch 6 (counts as first dc & ch-3), sc in next ch-3 sp, ch 3, *(3 sc, ch 5, 3 dc) in next ch-5 lp, ch 3, sc in next ch-3 sp, ch 3; rep from * once more, (3 sc, ch 5, 2 dc) in last lp; join with sl st to first dc (3rd ch of beg ch-6). (18 dc, 3 ch-5 lps, 3 sc & 6 ch-3 sps) Fasten off Color A and weave in all ends.

ROUND 3: With right side facing, join Color B with sl st to any ch-5 lp, ch 4, *wrap yarn twice around hook, insert hook in same lp, pull up lp, [yo, draw through 2 lps on hook] 2 times, rep from * once more (3 lps on hook), yo and draw through all 3 lps (first bobble made), ch 5, 3tr-bob in same lp, ch 5, 3 dc in next ch-3 sp, ch 1, 3 dc in next ch-3 sp, ch 5, *(3tr bob, ch 5, 3tr-bob in next ch-5 lp, ch 5, 3 dc in next ch-3 sp, ch 1, 3 dc in next ch-3 sp, ch 5; rep from * around; join with sl st to first tr (4th ch of beg ch-4) (6 bobbles, 18 dc, 3 ch-1 sps & 9 ch-5 lps)

ROUND 4: Sl st in next ch-5 lp, ch 3 (counts as first dc), [yo, insert hook in same lp, pull up lp, yo, draw through 2 lps on hook] 2 times (3 lps on hook), yo and draw through all 3 lps (first 3-bob made), ch 5, 3-bob in same lp, ch 5, sc in next ch-5 lp, ch 5, sc in next ch-1 sp, ch 5, sc in next ch-5 lp, ch 5, *(3-bob, ch 5, 3-bob) in next lp, ch 5, sc in next ch-5 lp, ch 5, sc in next ch-1 sp, ch 5, sc in next ch-5 lp, ch 5; rep from * around; join with sl st to first dc (3rd ch of beg ch-3). (6 bobbles, 9 sc & 15 ch-5 lps) Fasten off Color B and weave in all ends.

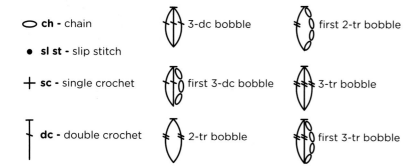

○ **ch -** chain

● **sl st -** slip stitch

+ **sc -** single crochet

╎ **dc -** double crochet

3-dc bobble

first 3-dc bobble

2-tr bobble

first 2-tr bobble

3-tr bobble

first 3-tr bobble

PATTERN

Base Round: Using Color A, ch 4; join with sl st to first ch to form a ring

ROUND 1: (Right Side) Ch 3 (counts as first dc, now and throughout), yo, insert hook in ring, pull up lp, yo, draw through 2 lps on hook (2 lps on hook), yo and draw through all lps (first 2-bob made), ch 3, [2-bob in ring, ch 3] 5 times; join with sl st to first dc (3rd ch of beg ch-3). (6 bobbles & 6 ch-3 sps) Fasten off and weave in all ends.

ROUND 2: With right side facing, join Color B with sl st to any ch-3 sp, ch 3, 2 dc in same sp, ch 3, [3 dc in next sp, ch 3] around; join with sl st to first dc (3rd ch of beg ch-3). (18 dc & 6 ch-3 sps) Fasten off Color B and weave in all ends.

ROUND 3: With right side facing, join Color C with sl st to any ch-3 sp, ch 4 (counts as first dc & ch-1, now and throughout), (dc, ch 1, dc, ch 3, dc, [ch 1, dc] 2 times) in same sp, ch 1, skip next dc, sc in next (center) dc, ch 1, skip next dc, *([dc, ch 1] 2 times, dc, ch 3, dc, [ch 1, dc] 2 times) in next ch-3 sp, ch 1, skip next dc, sc in next (center) dc, ch 1, skip next dc; rep from * around; join with sl st to first dc (3rd ch of beg ch-4). (6 petals) Fasten off Color C and weave in all ends.

ROUND 4: With right side facing, join Color D with sl st in any ch-3 sp, ch 4, (dc, ch 1, dc, ch 3, dc, [ch 1, dc] 2 times) in same sp, ch 2, sc in next sc, ch 2, *([dc, ch 1] 2 times, dc, ch 3, dc, [ch 1, dc] 2 times) in next ch-3 sp, ch 2, sc in next sc, ch 2; rep from * around; join with sl st to first dc (3rd ch of beg ch-4). (6 petals) Fasten off Color D and weave in all ends.

◯ **ch -** chain	✛ **sc -** single crochet	⧫ 2-dc bobble
• **sl st -** slip stitch	╪ **dc -** double crochet	⧫ first 2-dc bobble

MOTIF 41

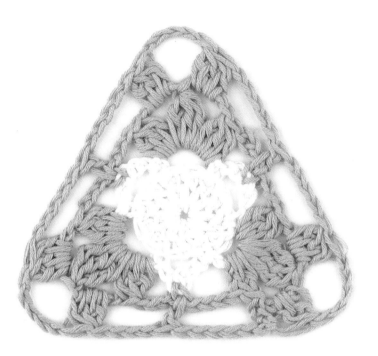

PATTERN

Base Round: Using Color A, ch 4; join with sl st to first ch to form a ring.

ROUND 1: (Right Side) Ch 3 (counts as first dc, now and throughout), 11 dc in ring; join with sl st to first dc (3rd ch of beg ch-3). (12 dc)

ROUND 2: Ch 1 (NOT counted as first st), sc in same st as joining, ch 5, skip next dc, *sc in next dc, ch 5, skip next dc; rep from * around; join with sl st to first sc. (6 sc & 6 ch-5 lps) Fasten off Color A and weave in all ends.

ROUND 3: With right side facing, join Color B with sl st to any ch-5 lp, ch 3, [yo, insert hook in same lp, pull up lp, yo, draw through 2 lps on hook] 2 times (3 lps on hook), yo and draw through all 3 lps (first 3-bob made), ch 4, (3tr-bob, ch 4, 3-bob) in same lp, ch 3, sc in next ch-5 lp, ch 3, *(3-bob, ch 4, 3tr-bob, ch 4, 3-bob) in next lp, ch 3, sc in next lp, ch 3; rep from * around; join with sl st to first dc (3rd ch of beg ch-3). (6 bobbles, 3 tr-bobbles, 3 sc, 6 ch-3 sps & 6 ch-4 lps)

ROUND 4: Sl st in next ch-4 sp, ch 3, [yo, insert hook in same lp, pull up lp, yo, draw through 2 lps on hook] 2 times (3 lps on hook), yo and draw through all 3 lps (first 3-bob made), ch 5, 3-bob in next ch-4 lp, ch 5, dc in next sc, ch 5, *[3-bob in next ch-4 lp, ch 5] 2 times, dc in next sc, ch 5; rep from * around; join with sl st to first dc (3rd ch of beg ch-3). (6 bobbles, 3 dc & 9 ch-5 lps) Fasten off Color B and weave in all ends.

○ ch - chain

● sl st - slip stitch

+ sc - single crochet

dc - double crochet

first 3-dc bobble

3-dc bobble

3-tr bobble

PATTERN

Base Round: Using Color A, ch 4; join with sl st to first ch to form a ring.

ROUND 1: (Right Side) Ch 1 (NOT counted as first st), 6 sc in ring; join with sl st to first sc. (6 sc)

ROUND 2: Ch 3 (counts as first dc, now and throughout), [yo, insert hook in same st as joining, pull up lp, yo, draw through 2 lps on hook] 2 times (3 lps on hook), yo and draw through all 3 lps (first 3-bob made), ch 5, *3-bob in next sc, ch 5; 3-bob in next sc, ch 3; rep from * around; join with sl st to first dc (3rd ch of beg ch-3). (6 bobbles & 6 ch-5 lps) Fasten off Color A and weave in all ends.

ROUND 3: With right side facing, join Color B with sl st to any ch-5 lp, ch 3, [yo, insert hook in same ch-5 lp, pull up lp, yo, draw through 2 lps on hook] 2 times (3 lps on hook), yo and draw through all 3 lps (first 3-bob made), ch 3, (tr, ch 3, 3-bob) in same lp, ch 3, sc in next ch-5 lp, ch 3, *(3-bob, ch 3, tr, ch 3, 3-bob) in next lp, ch 3, sc in next lp, ch 3; rep from * around; join with sl st to first dc (3rd ch of beg ch-3). (6 bobbles, 3 tr & 12 ch-3 sps) Fasten off Color B and weave in all ends.

ROUND 4: With right side facing, join Color C with sl st to first ch-3 sp (before tr), ch 3, 2 dc in same sp, *ch 3, 3 dc in next sp, [ch 1, 3 dc in next sp] 3 times; rep from * once more, ch 3, 3 dc in next sp, [ch 1, 3 dc in next sp] 2 times, ch 1; join with sl st to first dc (3rd ch of beg ch-3). (36 dc, 3 ch-3 sps & 9 ch-1 sps) Fasten off Color C and weave in all ends.

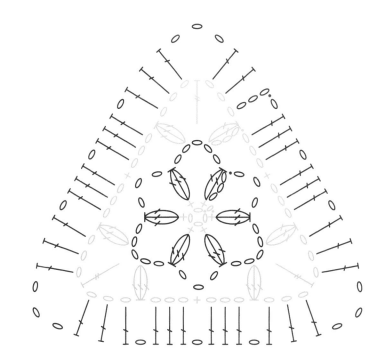

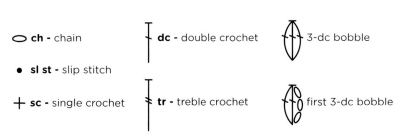

ch - chain
sl st - slip stitch
sc - single crochet
dc - double crochet
tr - treble crochet
3-dc bobble
first 3-dc bobble

MOTIF 43

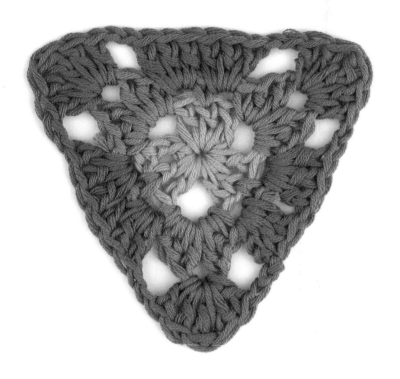

PATTERN

Base Round: Using Color A, ch 4; join with sl st to first ch to form a ring.

ROUND 1: (Right Side) Ch 3 (counts as first dc, now and throughout), 2 dc in ring, ch 3, [3 dc in ring, ch 3] 2 times; join with sl st to first dc (3rd ch of beg ch-3). (9 dc & 3 ch-3 sps) Fasten off Color A and weave in all ends.

ROUND 2: With right side facing, join Color B with sl st in center dc of any 3-dc group, ch 1 (NOT counted as first st), sc in same dc, ch 3, (sc, hdc, dc, ch 3, dc, hdc, sc) in next ch-3 sp, ch 3, * sc in center dc of next 3-dc group, ch 3, (sc, hdc, dc, ch 3, dc, hdc, sc) in next ch-3 sp, ch 3; rep from * around; join with sl st to first sc. (3 petals, 9 sc & 6 ch-3 sps) Fasten off and weave in all ends.

ROUND 3: With right side facing, join Color C with sl st to last ch-3 sp (before single sc), ch 3, 2 dc in same sp, 3 dc in next ch-3 sp, ch 2, (2 dc, tr, 2 dc) in next sp, ch 2, *3 dc in each of next 2 ch-3 sps, ch 2, (2 dc, tr, 2 dc) in next sp, ch 2; rep from * around; join with sl st to first dc (3rd ch of beg ch-3). (30 dc, 3 tr, & 6 ch-2 sps) Fasten off and weave in all ends.

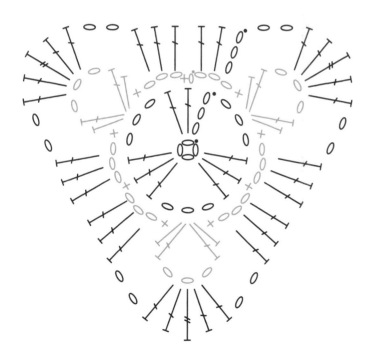

○ **ch -** chain   + **sc -** single crochet   **dc -** double crochet

● **sl st -** slip stitch   **hdc -** half double crochet   **tr -** treble crochet

PATTERN

Base Round: Using Color A, ch 4; join with sl st to first ch to form a ring.

ROUND 1: (Right Side) Ch 4 (counts as first tr), wrap yarn twice around hook, insert hook in ring, pull up lp, [yo, draw through 2 lps on hook] 2 times (2 lps on hook), yo and draw through both lps (first 2tr-bob made) ch 3, [2tr-bob in ring, ch 3] 5 times; join with sl st to first tr (4th ch of beg ch-4). (6 bobbles & 6 ch-3 sps) Fasten off Color A and weave in all ends.

ROUND 2: With right side facing, join Color B with sl st to any ch-3 sp, ch 1 (NOT counted as first st), sc in same sp, ch 7, sc in next ch-3 sp, ch 5, *sc in next sp, ch 7, sc in next sp, ch 5; rep from * around; join with sl st to first sc. (6 sc, 3 ch-7 lps & 3 ch-5 lps) Fasten off Color B and weave in all ends.

ROUND 3: With right side facing, join Color C with sl st to any ch-7 lp, ch 3 (counts as first dc), yo, insert hook in same ch-7 lp, pull up lp, yo, draw through 2 lps on hook (2 lps on hook), yo and draw through all lps (first 2-bob made), ch 1, (2-bob, ch 5, 2-bob, ch 1, 2-bob) in same sp, ch 3, sc in next ch-5 lp, ch 3, *(2-bob, ch 1, 2-bob, ch 5, 2-bob, ch 1, 2-bob) in same sp, ch 3, sc in next ch-5 lp, ch 3; rep from * around; join with sl st to first dc (3rd ch of beg ch-3). (12 bobbles, 3 sc, 6 ch-1 sp, 3 ch-5 lps & 6 ch-3 sps) Fasten off Color C and weave in all ends.

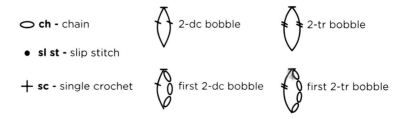

⬭ **ch -** chain

● **sl st -** slip stitch

✚ **sc -** single crochet

2-dc bobble

first 2-dc bobble

2-tr bobble

first 2-tr bobble

MOTIF 45

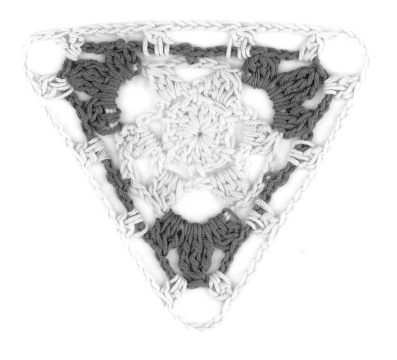

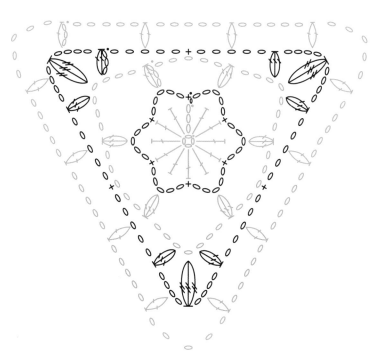

PATTERN

Base Round: Using Color A, ch 4; join with sl st to first ch to form a ring.

ROUND 1: (Right Side) Ch 3 (counts as first dc, now and throughout), 11 dc in ring; join with sl st to first dc (3rd ch of beg ch-3). (12 dc)

ROUND 2: Ch 1 (NOT counted as first st), sc in same st as joining, ch 5, skip next dc, [sc in next dc, ch 5, skip next dc] around; join with sl st to first sc. (6 sc & 6 ch-5 lps) Fasten off Color A and weave in all ends.

ROUND 3: With right side facing, join Color B with sl st to any ch-5 lp, ch 3, [yo, insert hook in same ch-5 lp, pull up lp, yo, draw through 2 lps on hook] 2 times (3 lps on hook), yo and draw through all 3 lps (first 3-bob made), ch 5, 3-bob in next ch-5 lp, ch 7, *3-bob in next lp, ch-5, 3 bob in next lp, ch 7; rep from * around; join with sl st to first dc (3rd ch of beg ch-3). (6 bobbles, 3 ch-5 lps & 3 ch-7 lps) Fasten off Color B and weave in all ends.

ROUND 4: With right side facing, join Color C with sl st to any ch-7 lp, ch 3, [yo, insert hook in same ch-7 lp, pull up lp, yo, draw through 2 lps on hook] 2 times (3 lps on hook), yo and draw through all 3 lps (first 3-bob made), ch 4, (3tr-bob, ch 4, 3-bob) in same lp, ch 5, sc in next ch-5 lp, ch 5, * (3 bob, ch 4, 3tr-bob, ch 4, 3-bob) in next ch-7 lp, ch 5, sc in next ch-5 lp, ch 5; rep from * around; join with sl st to first dc (3rd ch of beg ch-3) (9 bobbles, 3 sc, 6 ch-4 lps & 6 ch-5 lps) Fasten off Color C and weave in all ends.

ROUND 5: With right side facing, join Color D with sl st to first ch-4 lp (before tr-bob), ch 3, yo, insert hook in same lp, pull up lp, yo, draw through 2 lps on hook (3 lps on hook), yo and draw through all 3 lps (first 2-bob made), ch 5, *2-bob in next lp, ch 5; rep from * around; join with sl st to first dc (3rd ch of beg ch-3) (12 bobbles & 12 ch-5 lps) Fasten off Color D and weave in all ends.

⬭ **ch -** chain

● **sl st -** slip stitch

+ **sc -** single crochet

dc - double crochet

2-dc bobble

3-dc bobble

3-tr bobble

 first 2-dc bobble

 first 3-dc bobble

PATTERN

Base Round: Using Color A, ch 4; join with sl st to first ch to form a ring.

ROUND 1: (Right Side) Ch 6 (counts as first dc & ch-3), dc in ring, ch 5, *dc in ring, ch 3, dc in ring, ch 5; rep from * once more; join with sl st to first dc (3rd ch of beg ch-6). (6 dc, 3 ch-3 sps & 3 ch-5 lps) Fasten off Color A and weave in all ends.

ROUND 2: With right side facing, join Color B with sl st to any ch-5 lp, ch 3 (counts as first dc, now and throughout), (2 dc, ch 5, 3 dc) in same lp, ch 1, 3-bob in next ch-3 sp, ch 1, *(3 dc, ch 5, 3 dc) in next ch-5 lp, ch 1, 3-bob in next ch-3 sp, ch 1; rep from * around; join with sl st to first dc (3rd ch of beg ch-3). (18 dc, 3 bobbles, 6 ch-1 sps & 3 ch-5 lps) Fasten off Color B and weave in all ends.

ROUND 3: With right side facing, join Color C with sl st to any ch-5 lp, ch 3, (2 dc, ch 5, 3 dc) in same lp, [ch 2, 3-bob in next ch-1 sp] 2 times, ch 2, *(3 dc, ch 5, 3 dc) in next ch-5 lp, [ch 2, 3-bob in next ch-1 sp] 2 times, ch 2; rep from * around; join with sl st to first dc (3rd ch of beg ch-3). (18 dc, 6 bobbles, 18 ch-2 sps & 3 ch-5 lps) Fasten off Color C and weave in all ends.

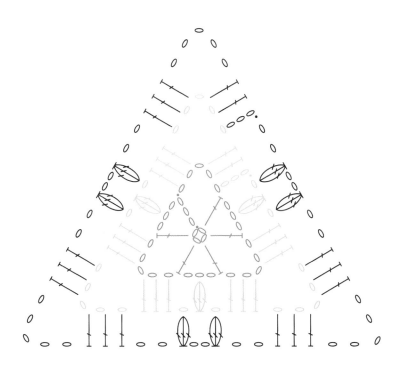

ch - chain   **dc -** double crochet   **3-dc bobble**

sl st - slip stitch

MOTIF 47

PATTERN

Base Round: Using Color A, ch 4; join with sl st to first ch to form a ring.

ROUND 1: (Right Side) Ch 3 (counts as first dc, now and throughout), 15 dc in ring; join with sl st to first dc (3rd ch of beg ch-3). (16 dc)

ROUND 2: Ch 3, dc in same st as joining, [2 dc in next dc] around; join with sl st to first dc (3rd ch of beg ch-3). (32 dc)

ROUND 3: Ch 1 (NOT counted as first st), sc in same st as joining, ch 11, sc in next dc, *sc in next dc, ch 11, sc in next dc; rep from * around; join with sl st to first sc. (32 sc & 16 ch-11 lps) Fasten off Color A and weave in all ends.

ROUND 4: With right side facing, join Color B with sl st to any ch-11 lp, ch 3, (2 dc, ch 3, 3 dc) in same lp, [(2 dc, ch 3, 3 dc) in next lp] around; join with sl st to first dc (3rd ch of beg ch-3). (16 shells) Fasten off and weave in all ends.

○ **ch -** chain   + **sc -** single crochet

● **sl st -** slip stitch   ⊥ **dc -** double crochet

PATTERN

Base Round: Using Color A, ch 4; join with sl st to first ch to form a ring,

ROUND 1: (Right Side) Ch 5 (counts as first dc & ch-2), [dc in ring, ch 2] 11 times; join with sl st to first dc (3rd ch of beg ch-5). (12 dc & 12 ch-2 sps)

ROUND 2: Sl st in next ch-2 sp, ch 4 (counts as first tr), *wrap yarn twice around hook, insert hook in same sp, pull up lp, [yo, draw through 2 lps on hook] 2 times, rep from * once more (3 lps on hook), yo and draw through all 3 lps (first 3tr-bob made), [ch 5, 3tr-bob in next ch-2 sp] 11 times, ch 2; join with dc to first tr (4th ch of beg ch-4). This makes the last ch-5 lp and positions yarn for next round. (12 bobbles & 12 ch-5 lps)

ROUND 3: Ch 3 (counts as first dc), yo, insert hook in ch-5 lp under joining, pull up lp, yo, draw through 2 lps on hook (3 lps on hook), yo and draw through all 3 lps (first 2-bob made), ch 3, 2-bob in same lp, ch 5, *(2-bob, ch 3, 2-bob) in next ch-5 lp, ch 5; rep from * around; join with sl st to first dc (3rd ch of beg ch-3). (24 bobbles, 12 ch-3 sps & 12 ch-5 lps) Fasten off and weave in all ends.

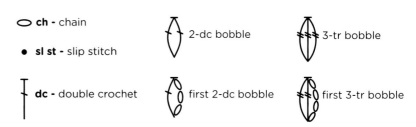

ch - chain

sl st - slip stitch

dc - double crochet

2-dc bobble

first 2-dc bobble

3-tr bobble

first 3-tr bobble

MOTIF 49

PATTERN

Base Round: Using Color A, ch 4; join with sl st to first ch to form a ring.

ROUND 1: (Right Side) Ch 4 (counts as first dc & ch-1, now and throughout), [dc in ring, ch 1] 11 times; join with sl st to first dc (3rd ch of beg ch-4). (12 dc & 12 ch-1 sps)

ROUND 2: Ch 3 (counts as first dc), yo, insert hook in same st as joining, pull up lp, yo, draw through 2 lps on hook (2 lps on hook), yo and draw through all lps (first 2-bob made), ch 7, [2-bob in next dc, ch 5] 2 times, *2-bob in next dc, ch 7, [2-bob in next dc, ch 5] 2 times; rep from * around; join with sl st to first dc (3rd ch of beg ch-3). (12 bobbles, 8 ch-5 lps & 4 ch-7 sps)

ROUND 3: Sl st in next ch-7 sp, ch 4, (dc, [ch 1, dc] 5 times) in same lp, ch 5, [sc in next ch-5 lp, ch 5] 2 times, *(dc, [ch 1, dc] 6 times) in same lp, ch 5, [sc in next ch-5 lp, ch 5] 2 times; rep from * around; join with sl st to first dc (3rd ch of beg ch-4). (28 dc, 24 ch-1 sps, 8 sc & 12 ch-5 lps)

ROUND 4: Ch 4, dc in next dc, [ch 1, dc in next dc] 5 times, ch 5, skip next ch-5 lp, sc in next ch-5 lp, ch 5, skip next ch-5 lp, *dc in next dc, [ch 1, dc in next dc] 6 times, ch 5, skip next ch-5 lp, sc in next ch-5 lp, ch 5, skip next ch-5 lp; rep from * around; join with sl st to first dc (3rd ch of beg ch 4). (28 dc, 24 ch-1 sps, 4 sc & 8 ch-5 lps) Fasten off and weave in all ends.

○ **ch -** chain   ✛ **sc -** single crochet   ◇ 2-dc bobble

● **sl st -** slip stitch   ┼ **dc -** double crochet   ◇ first 2-dc bobble

PATTERN

Base Round: Using Color A, ch 4; join with sl st to first ch to form a ring.

ROUND 1: (Right Side) Ch 3 (counts as first dc, now and throughout), 2 dc in ring, ch 3, 3 dc in ring, ch 3] 3 times; join with sl st to first dc (3rd ch of beg ch 3). (12 dc & 4 ch-3 sps) Fasten off Color A and weave in all ends.

ROUND 2: With right side facing, join Color B with sl st to any ch-3 sp, ch 3, (3 dc, ch 3, 4 dc) in same sp, ch 1, *(4 dc, ch 3, 4 dc) in next ch-3 sp, ch 1; rep from * around; join with sl st to first dc (3rd ch of beg ch-3). (24 dc, 4 ch-1 sps & 4 ch-3 sps) Fasten off Color B and weave in all ends.

ROUND 3: With right side facing, join Color A with sl st to any ch-3 sp, ch 3, yo, insert hook in sp, pull up lp, yo, draw through 2 lps on hook (2 lps on hook), yo and draw through all lps (first 2-bob made), [ch 3, 2-bob] 2 times in same sp, ch 5, sc in next ch-1 sp, ch 5, *(2-bob, [ch 3, 2-bob] 2 times) in next ch-3 sp, ch 5, sc in next ch-1 sp, ch 5; rep from * around; join with sl st to first dc (3rd ch of beg ch-3). (12 bobbles, 8 ch-3 sps, 4 sc & 8 ch-5 lps) Fasten off Color A and weave in all ends.

ROUND 4: With right side facing, join Color C with sl st to first ch-3 sp, ch 3, [yo, insert hook in same sp, pull up lp, yo, draw through 2 lps on hook] 2 times (3 lps on hook), yo and draw through all 3 lps (first 3-bob made), ch 3, 3-bob in next ch-3 sp, ch 5, [sc in next ch-5 lp, ch 5] 2 times, *3-bob in next ch-3 sp, ch 3, 3-bob in next ch-3 sp, ch 5, [sc in next ch-5 lp, ch 5] 2 times; rep from * around; join with sl st to first dc (3rd ch of beg ch-3). (8 bobbles, 4 ch-3 sps, 8 sc & 12 ch-5 lps).

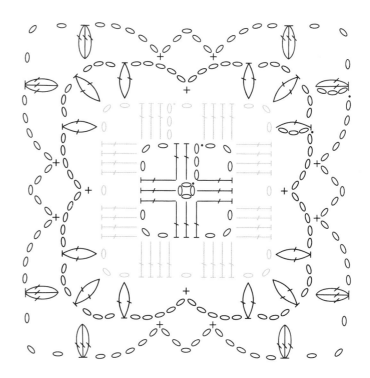

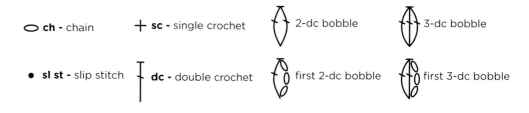

○ **ch** - chain   ┼ **sc** - single crochet   ◇ **2-dc bobble**   ◇ **3-dc bobble**

● **sl st** - slip stitch   ┼ **dc** - double crochet   ◇ **first 2-dc bobble**   ◇ **first 3-dc bobble**

PATTERN

Base Round: Using Color A, ch 4; join with sl st to first ch to form a ring.

ROUND 1: (Right Side) Ch 1 (NOT counted as first st), 6 sc in ring; join with sl st to first sc. (6 sc)

ROUND 2: Ch 4, (2tr-bob, ch 4, sl st) in same st as joining, *(sl st, ch 4, 2tr-bob, ch 4, sl st) in next sc; rep from * around; join with sl st to base of ch-4. (6 petals)

ROUND 3: Ch 8 (counts as first dc & ch-5), skip next petal, *dc between petals, ch 5, skip next petal; rep from * around; join with sl st to first dc (3rd ch of beg ch-8). (6 dc & 6 ch-5 lps)

ROUND 4: Ch 1, sc in same st as joining, (3 dc, ch 3, 3 dc) in next ch-5 lp, *sc in next dc, (3 dc, ch 3, 3 dc) in next ch-5 lp; rep from * around; join with sl st to first sc. (6 shells & 6 sc)

ROUND 5: Ch 6 (counts as first dc & ch-3), (2-bob, ch 3, 2-bob) in next ch-3 sp, ch 3, *dc in next sc, ch 3, (2-bob, ch 3, 2-bob) in next ch-3 sp, ch 3; rep from * around; join with sl st to first dc (3rd ch of beg ch-3). (12 bobbles, 6 dc & 18 ch-3 sps) Fasten off and weave in all ends.

⬭ **ch -** chain

● **sl st -** slip stitch

+ **sc -** single crochet

| **dc -** double crochet

⬨ **2-tr bobble**

⬨ **2-dc bobble**

MOTIF 52

3-Double Crochet Cluster (3dc-cl): Yo, insert hook into st or sp indicated, pull up lp (3 lps on hook), yo, draw through 2 lps on hook (2 lps on hook), *yo, insert hook in next st or sp, pull up lp, yo, draw through 2 lps on hook; rep from * once more (4 lps on hook), yo and draw through all 4 lps.

Note: The first Cluster Stitch in a round is started differently to subsequent cluster in round. Instructions for the first cluster are included within the pattern. For subsequent cluster follow the directions above.

PATTERN

Base Round: Using Color A, ch 4; join with sl st to first ch to form a ring.

ROUND 1: (Right Side) Ch 3 (counts as first dc, now and throughout), 2 dc in ring, ch 3, [3 dc in ring, ch 3] 3 times; join with sl st to first dc (3rd ch of beg ch 3). (12 dc & 4 ch-3 sps)

ROUND 2: Sl st in each of next 2 dc, sl st in next ch-3 sp, ch 3, (2 dc, ch 5, 3 dc) in same sp, ch 1, *(3 dc, ch 5, 3 dc) in next ch-3 sp, ch 1; rep from * around; join with sl st to first dc (3rd ch of beg ch-3). (24 dc, 4 ch-1 sps & 4 ch-5 lps)

ROUND 3: Ch 3, [yo, insert hook in next dc, pull up lp, yo, draw through 2 lps on hook] 2 times (3 lps on hook), yo and draw through all 3 lps (first cluster made), ch 1, (2-bob, ch 1, dc, ch 3, dc, ch 1, 2-bob) in next ch-5 lp, ch 1, *[3dc-cl (using next 3 dc), ch 1] 2 times, (2-bob, ch 1, dc, ch 3, dc, ch 1, 2-bob) in next ch-5 lp, ch 1; rep from * 2 times more, 3dc-cl (using next 3 dc), ch 1; join with sl st to first dc (3rd ch of beg ch-3). (8 bobbles, 8 clusters, 8 dc, 20 ch-1 sps & 4 ch-3 sps) Fasten off and weave in all ends.

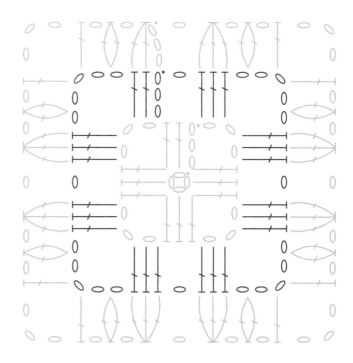

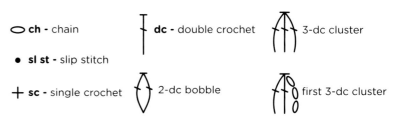

ch - chain   dc - double crochet   3-dc cluster

sl st - slip stitch

sc - single crochet   2-dc bobble   first 3-dc cluster

MOTIF 53

PATTERN

Base Round: Using Color A, ch 4; join with sl st to first ch to form a ring.

ROUND 1: (Right Side) Ch 1 (NOT counted as first st, now and throughout), 8 sc in ring; join with sl st to first sc. (8 sc)

ROUND 2: Ch 4 (counts as first tr), *wrap yarn twice around hook, insert hook in same st as joining, pull up lp, [yo, draw through 2 lps on hook] 2 times, rep from * once more (3 lps on hook), yo and draw through all 3 lps (first 3tr-bob made), ch 5, [3tr-bob in next sc, ch 5] around; join with sl st to first tr (4th ch of beg ch-4). (8 bobbles & 8 ch-5 lps) Fasten off Color A and weave in all ends.

ROUND 3: With right side facing, join Color B with sl st to any ch-5 lp, ch 1, sc in same lp, ch 5, [sc in next ch-5 lp, ch 5] around; join with sl st to first sc. (8 sc & 8 ch-5 lps)

ROUND 4: Sl st in next ch-5 lp, ch 3 (counts as first dc, (2 dc, ch 1, 3 dc) in same lp, ch 1, *(3 dc, ch 1, 3 dc) in same lp, ch 1; rep from * around; join with sl st to first dc (3rd ch of beg ch-3). (48 dc & 16 ch-1 sps) Fasten off Color B and weave in all ends.

ROUND 5: With right side facing, join Color C with sl st in any ch-1 sp, ch 1, (sc, ch 3, sc) in same sp, (sc in sp between next 2 dc) twice, skip next dc, *(sc, ch 3, sc) in next ch-1 sp, (sc in sp between next 2 dc) twice, skip next dc; rep from * around; join with sl st to first sc. (64 sc & 16 ch-3 sps) Fasten off Color C and weave in all ends.

⬮ **ch** - chain	┃ **dc** - double crochet
● **sl st** - slip stitch	**3-tr bobble**
✛ **sc** - single crochet	**3-tr bobble**

3-Double Crochet Cluster (3dc-cl): Yo, insert hook into st or sp indicated, pull up lp (3 lps on hook), yo, draw through 2 lps on hook (2 lps on hook), *yo, insert hook in next st or sp, pull up lp, yo, draw through 2 lps on hook; rep from * once more (4 lps on hook), yo and draw through all 4 lps.

Note: The first Cluster Stitch in a round is started differently to subsequent cluster in round. Instructions for the first cluster are included within the pattern. For subsequent cluster follow the directions above.

PATTERN

Base Round: Using Color A, ch 4; join with sl st to first ch to form a ring.

ROUND 1: (Right Side) Ch 1 (NOT counted as first st, now and throughout), [sc in ring, ch 3] 4 times; join with sl st to first sc. (4 sc & 4 ch-3 sps) Fasten off Color A and weave in all ends.

ROUND 2: With right side facing, join Color B with sl st to any ch-3 sp, ch 3 (counts as first dc, now and throughout), (dc, ch 1, 2 dc) in same sp, ch 1, *(2 dc, ch 1, 2 dc) in same sp, ch 1; rep from * around; join with sl st to first dc (3rd ch of beg ch-3). (16 dc & 8 ch-1 sps)

ROUND 3: Ch 3, yo, insert hook in next dc, pull up lp, yo, draw through 2 lps on hook, yo, insert hook in next ch-1 sp, pull up lp, yo, draw through 2 lps on hook (3 lps on hook), yo and draw through all 3 lps (first cluster made), ch 5, *3dc-cl (using same ch-1 sp and next 2 dc), ch 3, dc in next ch-1 sp, ch 3, 3dc-cl (using next 2 dc & next ch-1 sp), ch 5; rep from * 2 times more, 3dc-cl (using same ch-1 sp and next 2 dc), ch 3, dc in next ch-1 sp, ch 3; join with sl st to first dc (3rd ch of beg ch-3). (8 clusters, 4 dc, 8 ch-3 sps, & 4 ch-5 lps) Fasten off Color B and weave in all ends.

ROUND 4: With right side facing, join Color C with sl st to any ch-5 lp, ch 3, (2 dc, ch 3, 3 dc) in same lp, ch 1, skip next cluster, (2-bob, ch 2, 2-bob) in next dc, ch 1, *(3 dc, ch 3, 3 dc) in next ch-5 lp, ch 1, skip next cluster, (2-bob, ch 2, 2-bob) in next dc, ch 1; rep from * around; join with sl st to first dc (3rd ch of beg ch 3). (8 bobbles, 24 dc, 4 ch-3 sps, 4 ch-2 sps & ch-1 sps) Fasten off Color C and weave in all ends.

ROUND 5: With right side facing, join Color B with sl st to any ch-3 sp, ch 3, [yo, insert hook in same sp, pull up lp, yo, draw through 2 lps on hook] 2 times (3 lps on hook), yo and draw through all 3 lps (first 3-bob made), ch 3, 3-bob in same sp, ch 5, sc in next ch-1 sp, ch 3, sc in next ch-2 sp, ch 3, sc in next ch 1 sp, ch 5, *(3-bob, ch 3, 3-bob) in next ch-3 sp, ch 5, sc in next ch-1 sp, ch 3, sc in next ch-2 sp, ch 3, sc in next ch 1 sp, ch 5; rep from * around; join with sl st to first dc (3rd ch of beg ch-3). (8 bobbles, 8 sc, 12 ch-3 sps & 8 ch-5 lps) Fasten off and weave in all ends.

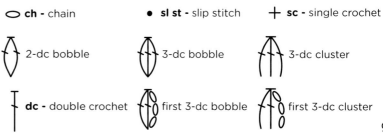

◯ **ch** - chain	● **sl st** - slip stitch	✛ **sc** - single crochet
2-dc bobble	3-dc bobble	3-dc cluster
dc - double crochet	first 3-dc bobble	first 3-dc cluster

MOTIF 55

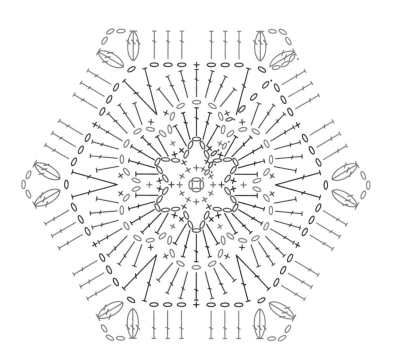

PATTERN

Base Round: Using Color A, ch 4; join with sl st to first ch to form a ring.

ROUND 1: (Right Side) Ch 1 (NOT counted as first st, now and throughout), 12 sc in ring; join with sl st to first sc. (12 sc)

ROUND 2: Ch 1, sc in same st as joining, ch 5, skip next sc, *sc in next sc, ch 5, skip next sc; rep from * around; join with sl st to first sc. (6 sc & 6 ch-5 lps) Fasten off Color A and weave in all ends.

ROUND 3: With right side facing, join Color B with sl st to any ch-5 lp, ch 1, (sc, hdc, 3 dc, hdc, sc) in same lp, *(sc, hdc, 3 dc, hdc, sc) in next ch-5 lp; rep from * around; join with sl st to first sc. (6 petals)

ROUND 4: Ch 1, sc in sp between petals, ch 7, skip next petal, *sc in next sp between petals, ch 7, skip next petal; rep from * around; join with sl st to first sc. (6 sc & 6 ch-7 lps) Fasten off Color B and weave in all ends.

ROUND 5: With right side facing, join Color C with sl st to any ch-7 sp, ch 1, (sc, hdc, 5 dc, hdc, sc) in same lp, *(sc, hdc, 5 dc, hdc, sc) in next lp; rep from * around; join with sl st to first sc. (6 petals) Fasten off Color C and weave in all ends.

ROUND 6: With right side facing, join Color D with sl st to sp between petals, ch 4 (counts as first dc & ch 1), dc in same sp, ch 3, sc in 3rd (center) dc of 5-dc group, ch 3, *(dc, ch 1, dc) in next sp between petals, ch 3, sc in next center dc, ch 3; rep from * around; join with sl st to first dc (3rd ch of beg ch-4). (12 dc, 6 ch-1 sp, 6 sc & 12 ch-3 sps)

ROUND 7: Sl st in first ch-1 sp, ch 3 (counts as first dc), [yo, insert hook in same sp, pull up lp, yo, draw through 2 lps on hook] 2 times (3 lps on hook), yo and draw through all 3 lps (first 3-bob made), ch 3, 3-bob in same sp, 3 dc in each of next 2 ch-3 sps, *(3 bob, ch 3, 3-bob) in next ch-1 sp, 3 dc in each of next 2 ch-3 sps; rep from * around; join with sl st to first dc (3rd ch of beg ch-3). (12 bobbles, 36 dc & 12 ch-3 sps) Fasten off Color D and weave in all ends.

 ch - chain

sl st - slip stitch

+ sc - single crochet

hdc - half double crochet

dc - double crochet

3-dc bobble

first 3-dc bobble

MOTIF 56

PATTERN

Base Round: Using Color A, ch 4; join with sl st to first ch to form a ring

ROUND 1: (Right Side) Ch 4 (counts as first dc & ch-1), [dc in ring, ch 1] 7 times; join with sl st to first dc (3rd ch of beg ch 4). (8 dc & 8 ch-1 sps) Fasten off Color A and weave in all ends.

ROUND 2: With right side facing, join Color B with sl st to any ch-1 sp, ch 1 (NOT counted as first st, now and throughout), (sc, ch 3, sc) in same sp, [(sc, ch 3, sc) in next ch-1 sp] around; join with sl st to first sc. (16 sc & 8 ch-3 sps) Fasten off Color B and weave in all ends.

ROUND 3: With right side facing, join Color C with sl st to any ch-3 sp, ch 3 (counts as first dc), (dc, ch 3, 2 dc) in same sp, ch 2, dc in next ch-3 sp, ch 2, *(2 dc, ch 3, 2 dc) in next sp, ch 2, dc in next sp, ch 2; rep from * around; join with sl st to first dc (3rd ch of beg ch-3). (20 dc, 16 ch-2 sps & 4 ch-3 sps) Fasten off Color C and weave in all ends.

ROUND 4: With right side facing, join Color D with sl st to any ch-3 sp, ch 1, (sc, ch 3, sc) in same sp, 2 sc in next 2 dc, [(sc, ch 3, sc) in next ch-2 sp] 2 times, sc in next dc, *(sc, ch 3, sc) in next ch-3 sp, sc in next dc, [(sc, ch 3, sc) in next ch-2 sp] 2 times, sc in next dc; rep from * around; join with sl st to first sc. (32 sc & 12 ch-3 sps) Fasten off Color D and weave in all ends.

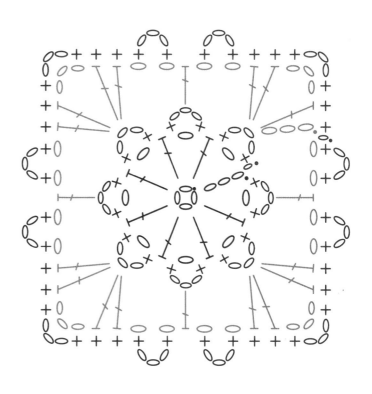

○ **ch** - chain   + **sc** - single crochet

● **sl st** - slip stitch   ┬ **dc** - double crochet

MOTIF 57

PATTERN

Base Round: Using Color A, ch 4; join with sl st to first ch to form a ring.

ROUND 1: (Right Side) Ch 5 (counts as first dc & ch-2), [dc in ring, ch 2] 7 times; join with sl st to first dc (3rd ch of beg ch-5). (8 dc & 8 ch-2 sps) Fasten off Color A and weave in all ends.

ROUND 2: With right side facing, join Color B with sl st to any ch-2 sp, ch 3 (counts as first dc, now and throughout), yo, insert hook in same sp, pull up lp, yo, draw through 2 lps on hook (2 lps on hook), yo and draw through all lps (first 2-bob made), ch 1, 2-bob in same sp, ch 1, *(2-bob, ch1, 2-bob) in next sp, ch 1; rep from * around; join with sl st to first dc (3rd ch of beg ch-3). (16 bobbles & 16 ch-1 sps) Fasten off Color B and weave in all ends.

ROUND 3: With right side facing, join Color C with sl st to any ch-1 sp, ch 1 (NOT counted as first st, now and throughout), sc in same sp, ch 3, *sc in next sp, ch 3; rep from * around; join with sl st to first sc. (16 sc & 16 ch-3 sps) Fasten off Color C and weave in all ends.

ROUND 4: With right side facing, join Color D with sl st to any ch-3 sp, ch 3, 2 dc in same sp, ch 1, *3 dc in next sp, ch 1; rep from * around; join with sl st to first dc (3rd ch of beg ch-3). (48 dc & 16 ch-1 sps) Fasten off Color D and weave in all ends.

ROUND 5: With right side facing, join Color B with sl st to any ch-1 sp, ch 1, sc in same sp, ch 5, *sc in next sp, ch 5; rep from * around; join with sl st to first sc. (16 sc & 16 ch-5 lps) Fasten off Color B and weave in all ends.

ROUND 6: With right side facing, join Color E with sl st to any ch-5 lp, ch 1, (2 sc, ch 3, 2 sc) in same sp, *(2 sc, ch 3, 2 sc) in next ch-5 lp; rep from * around; join with sl st to first sc. (64 sc & 16 ch-3 sps) Fasten off Color E and weave in all ends.

○ ch - chain	**+ sc** - single crochet	**2-dc bobble**
● sl st - slip stitch	**dc** - double crochet	**first 2-dc bobble** 

MOTIF 58

Popcorn (PC): 4 dc in same st or sp indicated, drop lp from hook, insert hook from front to back in first dc made, pull dropped lp through.

Note: The first Popcorn Stitch in a round is started differently to subsequent popcorns in round. Instructions for the first popcorns are included within the pattern. For subsequent popcorns follow the directions above.

PATTERN

Base Round: Using Color A, ch 4; join with sl st to first ch to form a ring.

ROUND 1: (Right Side) Ch 1 (NOT counted as first st, now and throughout), 8 sc in ring; join with sl st to first sc. (8 sc) Fasten off Color A and weave in all ends.

ROUND 2: With right side facing, join Color B with sl st to any sc, ch 3 (counts as first dc, now and throughout), 3 dc in same st, drop lp from hook, insert hook from front to back in first dc (3rd ch of beg ch-3), pull dropped lp through (first popcorn made), ch 2, *PC in next sc, ch 2; rep from * around; join with sl st to first dc (3rd ch of beg ch-3). (8 popcorns & 8 ch-2 sps) Fasten off Color B and weave in all ends.

ROUND 3: With right side facing, join Color C with sl st to any ch-2 sp, ch 3, 3 dc in same sp, ch 1, *4 dc in next ch-2 sp, ch 1; rep from * around; join with sl st to first dc (3rd ch of beg ch-3). (32 dc & 8 ch-1 sps) Fasten off Color C and weave in all ends.

ROUND 4: With right side facing, join Color D with sl st to any ch-1 sp, ch 1, scin same sp, ch 5, *sc in next ch-1 sp, ch 5; rep from * around; join with sl st to first sc. (8 sc & 8 ch-5 lps) Fasten off Color D and weave in all ends.

ROUND 5: With right side facing, join Color C with sl st to any ch-5 lp, ch 3, 4 dc in same lp, ch 1, *5 dc in next lp, ch 1; rep from * around; join with sl st to first dc (3rd ch of beg ch-3). (40 dc & 8 ch-1 sps) Fasten off Color C and weave in all ends.

ROUND 6: With right side facing, join Color D with sl st to center dc of any 5-dc group, ch 1, sc in same st, ch 3, skip next 2 dc, sc in next ch-1 sp, ch 3, skip next 2 dc, *sc in next (center) dc, ch 3, skip next 2 dc, sc in next ch-1 sp, ch 3, skip next 2 dc; rep from * around; join with sl st to first sc. (16 sc & 16 ch-3 sps) Fasten off Color D and weave in all ends.

ROUND 7: With right side facing, join Color E with sl st to any ch-3 sp, ch 1, (2 sc, ch 3, 2 sc) in same sp, *(2 sc, ch 3, 2 sc) in next ch-3; rep from * around; join with sl st to first sc. (64 sc & 16 ch-3 sps) Fasten off and weave in all ends. Fasten off.

⬭ **ch** - chain

● **sl st** - slip stitch

✛ **sc** - single crochet

╪ **dc** - double crochet

⬭ **pc** - popcorn stitch

⬭ **first popcorn stitch**

MOTIF 59

PATTERN

Base Round: Using Color A, ch 4; join with sl st to first ch to form a ring.

ROUND 1: (Right Side) Ch 1 (NOT counted as first st, now and throughout), 8 sc in ring; join with sl st to first sc. (8 sc) Fasten off Color A and weave in all ends.

ROUND 2: With right side facing, join Color B with sl st to any sc, ch 1, sc in same st, ch 4, 3tr-bob in next sc, ch 4, *sc in same sc, ch 4, 3tr-bob in next sc, ch 4; rep from * around; join with sl st to first sc. (4 bobbles, 4 sc & 8 ch-4 lps) Fasten off Color B and weave in all ends.

ROUND 3: With right side facing, join Color C with sl st to any sc, ch 8 (counts as first dc & ch-5, now and throughout), sc in next bobble, ch 5, *dc in next sc, ch 5, sc in next bobble, ch 5; rep from * around; join with sl st to first dc (3rd ch of beg ch-8). (4 dc, 4 sc & 8 ch-5 lps) Fasten off Color C and weave in all ends.

ROUND 4: With right side facing, join Color D with sl st to any sc, ch 8, dc in same sc, ch 3, sc in next ch-5 lp, ch 3, 3-bob in next dc, ch 3, sc in next ch-5 lp, ch 3, *(dc, ch 5, dc) in next sc, ch 3, sc in next ch-5 lp, ch 3, 3-bob in next dc, ch 3, sc in next ch-5 lp, ch 3; rep from * around; join with sl st to first dc (3rd ch of beg ch-8). (4 bobbles, 8 dc, 8 sc, 16 ch-3 sps & 4 ch-5 lps) Fasten off Color D and weave in all ends.

ROUND 5: With right side facing, join Color E with sl st to any ch-5 lp, ch 1, (2 sc, ch 5, 2 sc) in same lp, [(sc, ch 3, sc) in next ch-3 sp] 4 times, *(2 sc, ch 5, 2 sc) in next ch-5 lp, [(sc, ch 3, sc) in next ch-3 sp] 4 times; rep from * around; join with sl st to first sc. (48 sc, 16 ch-3 sps & 4 ch-5 lps) Fasten off Color E and weave in all ends.

○ **ch -** chain   + **sc -** single crochet   ⬙ 3-dc bobble

• **sl st -** slip stitch   ┆ **dc -** double crochet   ⬙ 3-tr bobble

MOTIF 60

PATTERN

Base Round: Using Color A, ch 4; join with sl st to first ch to form a ring.

ROUND 1: (Right Side) Ch 6 (counts as first dc & ch 3, now and throughout), [dc in ring, ch 3] 5 times; join with sl st to first dc (3rd ch of beg ch-6). (6 dc & 6 ch-3 sps)

ROUND 2: Sl st in first ch-3 sp, ch 3 (counts as first dc, now and throughout), 3 dc in same sp, ch 3, [4 dc in next ch-3 sp, ch 3] around; join with sl st to first dc (3rd ch of beg ch-3). (24 dc & 6 ch-3 sps)

ROUND 3: Ch 6, skip next dc group, [(2 dc, ch 3, 2 dc) in next ch-3 sp, ch 3] 5 times, (2 dc, ch 3, dc) in last ch-3 sp; join with sl st to first dc (3rd ch of beg ch-6). (24 dc & 12 ch-3 sps)

ROUND 4: Sl st in first ch-3 sp, ch 3, 3 dc in same sp, ch 1, (2 dc, ch 3, 2 dc) in next ch-3 sp, ch 1, *4 dc in next ch-3 sp, ch 1, (2 dc, ch 3, 2 dc) in next ch-3 sp, ch 1; rep from * around; join with sl st to first dc (3rd ch of beg ch-3). (48 dc, 6 ch-3 sps & 12 ch-1 sps)

ROUND 5: Ch 1 (NOT counted as first st, now and throughout), sc in same st as joining, [sc in next st or sp] around, working 3 sc in each corner ch-3 sp; join with sl st to first sc. (78 sc) Fasten off and weave in all ends.

ROUND 6: With right side facing, join Color B with sl st to any sc, ch 1, sc in each sc around; join with sl st to first sc. (78 sc) Fasten off Color B and weave in all ends.

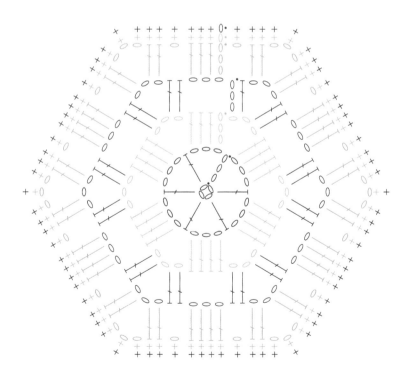

⬭ **ch -** chain	+ **sc -** single crochet
• **sl st -** slip stitch	╀ **dc -** double crochet

MAGIC RING (OR ADJUSTABLE RING)

1 Form a loop with the yarn, keeping the tail end of the yarn behind the working yarn (the yarn attached to the ball).

2 Insert the hook through the loop (from front to back), and pull the working yarn through the loop (from back to front). Do not tighten up the loop.

3 Using the working yarn, make a chain stitch (to secure the ring). This chain stitch does NOT count as first stitch.

4 Work the required stitches into the ring (over the tail strand). When all the stitches are done, gently tug the tail end to close the ring, before joining the round (if specified). Remember, make sure this tail is firmly secured before weaving in the end.

Note If you prefer, you can use any type of "ring" to start your project (or start with ch-2, and working the first round in the second chain from hook). The advantage of using the adjustable Magic Ring, is that when it is tightened, it closes the hole completely.

Tip Secure your Magic Ring after the first few rounds and before you start stuffing.

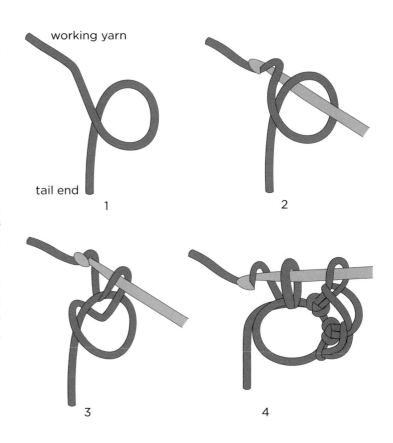

working yarn

tail end

1

2

3

4

SLIP KNOT

Create a loop with your yarn, making sure that the tail end is hanging behind your loop. Insert the hook through the loop, and pick up the ball end of the yarn.

Draw yarn through loop and pull on tail end gently to create slip knot on hook.

SLIP STITCH (SL ST)

This stitch does not add height to your work and is most commonly used to move to a different position or for joining.

To start, insert the hook into the indicated stitch or space. Yarn over hook and draw through stitch or space and the loop on hook.

CHAIN

Nearly all crochet projects start with a series of chain stitches, as well as being used within stitch patterns. It is important to keep your tension even so the stitches are neither too tight nor too loose.

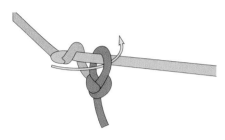

Start with a slip knot on your hook. Wrap yarn over hook and draw through loop on hook to complete chain stitch.

SINGLE CROCHET (SC)

This is the shortest of the crochet stitches and one of the easiest and most commonly used stitches.

Start by inserting your hook into the indicated stitch or space. Wrap yarn over hook and draw through stitch or space. There are now 2 loops on the hook.

Wrap yarn over hook and draw through both loops to complete the stitch.

HALF DOUBLE CROCHET (HDC)

This stitch is halfway in height between a single crochet and double crochet.

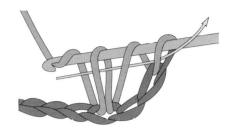

Start by wrapping yarn over hook once and then inserting hook into the indicated stitch or space. Wrap yarn over hook again and draw loop through. There are nor 3 loops on the hook. Wrap yarn over hook and draw through all 3 loops to complete the stitch.

SINGLE CROCHET DECREASE - (SC2TOG)

Insert hook in next stitch and pull up a loop, (two loops on hook). Insert hook in next stitch and pull up a loop (three loops on hook). Yarn over, draw through all three loops on hook.

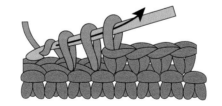

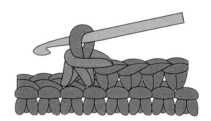

JOIN WITH SINGLE CROCHET

With slip knot on hook, insert hook in st or sp indicated, pull up lp (2 lps on hook), yo, draw through both loops on hook (first single crochet made).

DOUBLE CROCHET (DC)

This stitch is the other most commonly used stitch. It is a taller stitch that creates a softer, more open fabric.

Start by wrapping yarn over hook once and then inserting hook into the indicated stitch or space. Wrap yarn over hook again and draw loop through. There are now 3 loops on the hook.

Wrap yarn over hook again and draw through both loops to complete the stitch.

Wrap yarn over hook and draw through first 2 loops.

TREBLE (OR TRIPLE) CROCHET (TR)

This stitch is taller than double crochet and is often used in decorative stich patterns or to add height to corners.

Start by wrapping yarn over hook twice and then inserting hook into the indicated stitch or space.

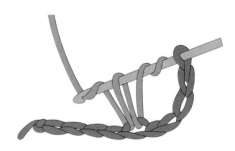

Wrap yarn over hook and draw loop through. There are now 4 loops on the hook.

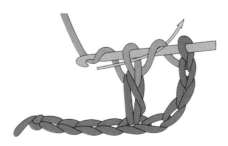

Wrap yarn over hook and draw through first 2 loops. There are now 3 loops on the hook. Wrap yarn over hook and draw through 2 loops on hook. There are now 2 loops on the hook.

Wrap yarn over and draw through remaining 2 loops to complete the stitch.

DOUBLE TREBLE (DTR)
TRIPLE TREBLE (TTR)

These stitches are worked in the same way as a treble stitch. The stitch height is altered by the amount of times you wrap the yarn around your hook at the beginning of the stitch.

A double treble is started by wrapping yarn over hook 3 times.

A triple treble is started by wrapping yarn over hook 4 times.

The stitch is then completed in the same way as a treble by wrapping yarn over hook and drawing through 2 loops at a time until the end.

PUFF STITCHES

A puff stitch is similar to a bobble stitch but is made using half double crochet stitches and is smoother and plumper than a bobble.

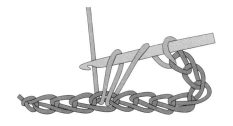

Start by making an incomplete half double crochet stitch (i.e. don't complete the final stage of drawing yarn through last 3 loops. When starting each new half double crochet, draw the loop up higher than normal.

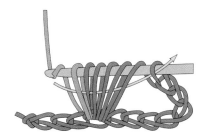

Once the required number of stitches have been made, draw yarn through all loops on hook.

Normally this stitch will be secured by a chain stitch. However this will vary according to the pattern. Check the pattern instructions first.

SHELLS

This stitch is most often used as a decorative scalloped border and is generally made using taller stitches such as double or treble crochet.

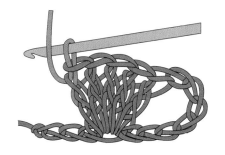

Shells are formed by working a number of stitches into the same point.

To make a shell, work the specified number of stitches into the same space.

CLUSTERS (CL)

Clusters are the reverse of a shell in that a number of stitches are worked before joining together at the top. This creates a shell that fans out downwards.

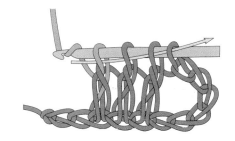

To make a double crochet cluster, work the stitch as normal but stopping at the final step of drawing yarn through last 2 loops. Keep these loops on hook and make a double crochet in the next stitch, but stopping before the final step. Continue working this way for the required amount of stitches.

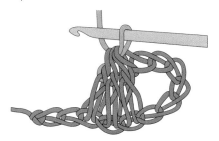

Once you have all your stitches made, yarn over hook and draw through all loops to complete cluster.

BOBBLES

Bobbles are a textural stitch, giving your work a raised surface. They are worked in a similar way to a cluster except that all the stitches are worked into the same space.

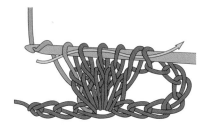

Work your stitches as normal but stop at the final step of drawing yarn through last 2 loops. Keep these loops on your hook and start the next double crochet, into the same stitch but stopping before the final step. Continue working this way until the required amount of stitches have been made.

Normally a bobble will be secured at the top by a chain stitch. However some patterns may specify not to complete this step. Always check the pattern whether this step in required.

2-Double Crochet Bobble (2-bob): Yo, insert hook into st or sp indicated, pull up lp, yo, draw through 2 lps on hook, yo, insert hook in same st or sp, pull up lp, yo, draw through 2 lps on hook (3 lps on hook), yo and draw through all 3 lps.

3-Double Crochet Bobble (3-bob): Yo, insert hook into st or sp indicated, pull up lp, yo, draw through 2 lps on hook, [yo, insert hook in same st or sp, pull up lp, yo, draw through 2 lps on hook] 2 times more (4 lps on hook), yo and draw through all 4 lps.

4-Double Crochet Bobble (4-bob): Yo, insert hook into st or sp indicated, pull up lp, yo, draw through 2 lps on hook, [yo, insert hook in same st or sp, pull up lp, yo, draw through 2 lps on hook] 3 times more (5 lps on hook), yo and draw through all 5 lps.

2-Treble Bobble (2tr-bob): Wrap yarn twice around hook, insert hook into st or sp indicated, pull up lp (4 lps on hook), [yo, draw through 2 lps on hook] 2 times (2 lps on hook), wrap yarn twice around hook, insert hook in same st or sp, pull up lp, [yo, draw through 2 lps on hook] 2 times (3 lps on hook), yo and draw through all 3 lps.

3-Treble Bobble (3tr-bob): Wrap yarn twice around hook, insert hook into st or sp indicated, pull up lp (4 lps on hook), [yo, draw through 2 lps on hook] 2 times (2 lps on hook), *wrap yarn twice around hook, insert hook in same st or sp, pull up lp, [yo, draw through 2 lps on hook] 2 times, rep from * once more (4 lps on hook), yo and draw through all 4 lps.

4-Treble Bobble (4tr-bob): Wrap yarn twice around hook, insert hook into st or sp indicated, pull up lp (4 lps on hook), [yo, draw through 2 lps on hook] 2 times (2 lps on hook), *wrap yarn twice around hook, insert hook in same st or sp, pull up lp, [yo, draw through 2 lps on hook] 2 times, rep from * 2 times more (5 lps on hook), yo and draw through all 5 lps.

Note: The first Bobble Stitch in a round is started differently to subsequent bobbles in round. Instructions for the first bobble are included within the pattern. For subsequent bobbles follow the directions above.

POPCORNS

This stitch is similar to a shell but it is drawn together at the top to create surface texture.

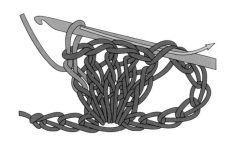

Work the required number of stitches into the same space. When the last stitch has been completed, remove hook and insert into the top of the first stitch of the group, pick up dropped loop.

Yarn over hook, draw through both loops to complete.

The completed popcorn will sit away from the surface of your work.

PICOT STITCH

The picot stitch is mainly used as a decorative stitch for edging blankets etc in this book I use it as a shaping stitch to create a point on leaves.

Chain 3, insert your hook back into the top of the stitch you are working from, yarn over and pull through all loop.

 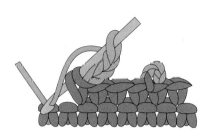

FRONT AND BACK LOOPS

Every stitch has what looks like 'v's on the top. There are two loops that make up the 'v'. The front loop is the loop closest to you and the back loop is the loop furthest from you. Generally, we work in both loops – under both the front and back loops. Working in either the front or back loops only, creates a decorative ridge (made up of the unworked loops).

Back Loop Both Loops Front Loop

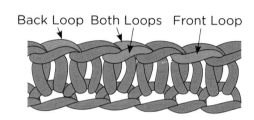

CROCHETING AROUND A WIRE STEM

1. Fold the ends of the wire to make a place to attach the yarn and so any sharp cut ends are hidden.

2. Attach the yarn and work double crochet around the stem in the same way you would work into a magic ring or chain space. You can bend the wire to make it easier to work around.

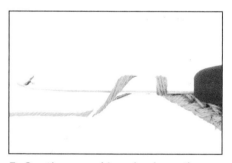

3. Continue working dc along the stem, making sure the stem is covered.

4. Attach the flowers, by tying or stitching them into place, any knots will be covered by the crochet on the stem.

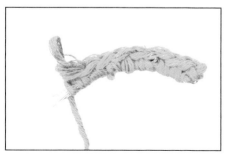

5. You can use the same technique to quickly create leaves.

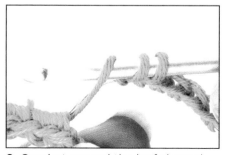

6. Crochet around the leaf shaped wire in the same way, joining with a ss at the end.

┬ - treble crochet
○ chain
× single crochet
╪ double crochet
┬ half double crochet
• slip stitch
⊗ 3 bobble stitch

MOTIF NR. 9